everyday
ROSES

everyday

HOW TO GROW KNOCK OUT® AND OTHER EASY-CARE GARDEN ROSES

ROSES

Paul Zimmerman

The Taunton Press

For Pam: The most beautiful rose God created.

Text © 2013 by Paul Zimmerman
Photographs © 2013 by Rob Cardillo, except as noted on p. 181

This work of *Everyday Roses*, ISBN 978-1-60085-778-2, is published with grateful acknowledgment
to Star® Roses and Plants/Conard-Pyle for their contributions to the book.

 The Taunton Press
Inspiration for hands-on living®

The Taunton Press, Inc., 63 South Main Street, PO Box 5506, Newtown, CT 06470-5506
e-mail: tp@taunton.com

Editor: Renee Iwaszkiewicz Neiger
Copy editor: Betty Christiansen
Indexer: Barbara Mortenson
Jacket/Cover design: Carol Singer / notice design
Interior design: Rita Sowins/Sowins Design
Layout: Rita Sowins/Sowins Design

The following names/manufacturers appearing in Everyday Roses are trademarks: Abbaye de Cluny™,
The Alnwick®, Biltmore®, Biltmore Naturals™, Black Forest™, Bolero™, Brite Eyes™, Brothers Grimm™,
Cancan™, Carefree Delight™, Carefree Spirit™, Carefree Sunshine™, Carefree Wonder™, Climbing Eden™,
David Austin®, Dawn®, Drift®, Earth-Kind®, Easy Elegance®, Eden Climber™, Felco®, Flamingo Kolorscape™,
Home Run®, Jean Giono™, Knock Out®, The Knock Out® Family of Roses, Kordes Golden Gate™, Mandarin Ice™,
Marjorie Fair®, Meidiland®, Morning Magic™, Mystic Fairy®, Orchid Romance™, Oso Easy®, Oso Happy™,
Proven Winners®, Raspberry Cream Twirl™, Romantica®, Roxy™, Solero Vigorosa®, Star® Roses and Plants/
Conard-Pyle, Traviata™, Winners Circle™, White Eden™

Library of Congress Cataloging-in-Publication Data

Zimmerman, Paul, 1958-
  Everyday roses : how to grow Knock Out® and other easy-care garden roses / Paul Zimmerman.
      p. cm.
  Every day roses
  How to grow Knock Out? and other easy-care garden roses
  Includes index.
  ISBN 978-1-60085-778-2
1. Roses--United States. 2. Roses--Varieties--United States. I. Title. II. Title: Every day roses. III. Title: How to
grow Knock Out? and other easy-care garden roses.
  SB411.Z56 2013
  635.9'33734--dc23
                            2012047103

Printed in the United States of America
10 9 8 7 6 5 4 3 2 1

Acknowledgments

"I don't know whether nice people tend to grow roses, or growing roses makes people nice." –*Roland A. Brown, American professor*

Being a first-time author, I have no experience thanking the people who have in their own ways made it possible for me to write this book. So I'll just jump right in.

Mr. Freer, my high school AP history teacher, who taught me how to learn as opposed to memorize. Steve Jones for showing that slide of Somebreuil that spun me into the world of old garden roses. Michael Marriott for his thoughts on garden design and his orange marmalade recipe. David Stone for sharing his amazing gardening skills and for lovely talks with him and his wife, Ann, during soft fall evenings on our front porch. All my customers of Hundred Acre Woods in Los Angeles, who let me play and learn in their gardens. Clair Martin for allowing me to run rampant in the rose study plot of the Huntington Botanical Gardens. Kim Rupert for being Kim Rupert. Marily Williams for letting me tag along in the Fineschi Garden. Tom Carruth, Ralph Moore, and the other rose nursery people so generous with their time and knowledge.

To everyone who helped and encouraged me along the way, and you know you who you are.

Tommy Cairns for taking me under his wing and teaching me a great deal of what I know about rose horticulture and for giving me room to find my own ideas—also to him and his partner, Luis Desemaro, for some killer dinner parties. Bob Edberg for all those hours under that tree at Limberlost Roses and for allowing me access to his rose library. Mike and Irene Lowe, without whom Ashdown Roses would never have been. Sue Hopkins and Marji Lynn, you crazy kids. Darren Gilbert, Parker Andes, Tim Rosebrock, and the gang at Biltmore® for their partnership and a beautiful place to stop and smell the roses. Dirck, Mark, and John,

the "Organics Boys." Everyone at Bierkreek Nursery for being so ahead of the curve. Bud Meyer for being a great person and mentor. Phillip Hess for invaluable legal counsel, his knowledge of wine, and the wonderful friendship I have with him and his wife, Margaret. The art and production staff at The Taunton Press for making this book look good. Shawna Mullen and Renee Neiger, my editors at Taunton Press, for pushing this through and leading this first-time book author through the maze of "how do we do that?"

Father Michael Doty and my Holy Cross family. Steve Hutton at Star® Roses and Plants/Conard-Pyle not only for backing this project but also for his vision of what garden roses should be. Everyone who contributed photos and thoughts to this book. My Ashdown family. Clifford Orent for being as over-the-top about roses as I am and most of all for being a great friend, sounding board, and supporter. The entire Beales family: Amanda for her roses, Richard for his friendship and can-do attitude, Joan for those morning warm cups of tea, and of course, the entire Beales family for those lovely pub dinners. But particularly to Peter for his confidence, his encouragement in what I was doing, his befriending someone new in roses that he barely knew, and for teaching me how to play snooker. Trish Walsh for holding down the fort at Ashdown while I went off on my tangents. This book wouldn't exist without you. To all the "Makers of Heavenly Roses"—without your rose-breeding talent, this book would have been pointless.

But more than anyone else, thanks to my nieces, nephews, sisters, my mother, my late father, and my partner of 20-plus years, Pam, for not thinking I was totally nuts—at least that's what they said to my face.

Contents

Foreword

I first met Paul at the Huntington Botanical Gardens in Pasadena, California, 12 years ago. I had just delivered a lecture, and Paul was one of the audience members who asked questions of me at the end. It was not difficult to ascertain from the questions he asked that he was a man who already knew quite a lot about our shared subject, but he was keen to learn even more. Since then, Paul and I have become close friends, and I have come to respect his knowledge of the subject to the point where I now ask him questions and have learned to respect his answers as being accurate, straightforward, and to the point. It is these three features that best sum up Paul's work in this book. This said, there is a danger that such adjectives could imply a dull, dry read; far from it. For Paul has the ability to use his command of the English language to bring even the dullest of items to life.

Another word that springs to mind from reading this book is *enthusiasm*, for it is impossible to read more than two or three pages without realizing that it is written by a man in love with his subject and who wishes to impart this love to his readers. *Refreshing* is another word that amply describes Paul's approach to his subject. It's refreshing because he challenges lots of the old, established methods of growing roses, not to mention that he possesses a readiness to express firmly held opinions about types and cultivars, which will make some of the "old school" rose growers raise their eyebrows! I didn't need to raise mine, as without exception, I agree wholeheartedly with everything he has written.

At this point, I feel that a direct quote is appropriate: "I hope in its own way, this book will teach you that you can grow roses sustainably using simple techniques and your own gardener's instincts, all applied with a healthy dose of common sense." As a nurseryman in touch with gardeners and rose growers on a daily basis, I feel it would be a good idea for me to copy this quotation and display it for all to see in my sales office.

Another element of Paul's philosophy with which I concur is avoiding the use of chemicals for disease and pest control. I know that, like me, Paul loves old garden roses, but sadly, quite a few of the beautiful oldies are rather more prone to disease than some of modern cultivars, such as the Knock Out rose. Paul goes into considerable detail on chemical-free disease control. And one thing that becomes clear is that there are many modern roses that are very disease resistant. However, if your taste is for the older cultivars, avoid the use of chemicals from the start and these grand old roses will build up their own resistance to ill health and will take their rightful place along modern garden roses.

To conclude, I believe that anyone who reads this book and follows Paul's philosophy cannot help but have a garden of healthy roses and furthermore, by so doing, will get tremendous pleasure from the experience.

—*Peter Beales, author and rose expert*

Paul Zimmerman (left) and Peter Beales (right).

2

Preface

I've always felt most gardeners would love to add roses to their home landscape. Yet they don't for one of two reasons. Either they tried growing roses, felt they were too complicated, and gave up, or they always heard roses were difficult and never tried to grow them in the first place. If that sounds familiar (or if you have purchased garden roses like the Knock Out rose and noticed the "traditional" rose-care methods don't apply to them) then this book is for you.

You've all read or heard the "rules" (and if you haven't, consider yourselves among the lucky). Fertilization programs that call for myriad ingredients—most of them smelly—that need to be applied at the precise time, in an exact amount, using only a sprayer made from self-sanitizing plutonium. Deadheading done only to five-leaflet leaf sets that have bud eyes facing outward—or are at least facing magnetic north. Planting distances spaced within NASA-tolerant variances, in soil sterilized of all life and cleared of any encroaching perennial, bulb, or annual. Pruning techniques that are draconian in their method and designed only to achieve long stems for cutting, and, of course, an arsenal of chemicals best viewed through the mask of a hazmat suit.

Sound ridiculous? While I've taken the above well beyond the extreme, after many years in roses, I've ceased being amazed at how complicated some "rose experts" can make what is truly a lovely, relaxing, and beautiful hobby. And that is simply what rose growing is to the vast majority who garden—a delightful hobby.

You see, The Knock Out Family of Roses are garden roses, and garden roses are nothing more than flowering shrubs. That's it in a nutshell. They are not the fussy roses that your grandmother may have grown and spent all of her weekends caring for. There are lots of great garden roses out there just like Knock Out roses that are easy to grow and use in the general landscape. I know this for a fact because I grow hundreds of roses in my own no-chemical garden with great success. Some are old, dating back hundreds of years, and some are brand new. If you are skeptical, note this one fact: Modern agricultural chemicals didn't exist before the 1930s and weren't widely available to homeowners until the 1950s. Yet roses have been in commerce for hundreds of years. So roses were grown and thrived without chemicals far longer than with them.

About 15 years ago, I obtained the book *Roses for Every Garden* by R. C. Allen (M. Barrows, 1962), whose reasons for writing it ring true to me today. I quote from Mr. Allen's foreword both because he says it so well and to acknowledge the influence of those who have gone before: "Somehow, the idea that roses are difficult has crept into our horticultural thinking, perhaps because we expect greater perfection from roses than from other flowers. Then in our efforts to excel we have made rose growing laborious, time consuming, even costly and lost the recreation and inspiration that more modest aims can provide."

Mr. Allen wrote those words in 1948, and they are still relevant today. But as Bob Dylan said, "The times they are a-changin.'" Roses like Knock Out are showing gardeners that they, too, can grow roses without fuss. The "green" movement throughout the world is thankfully creating demand for plants grown without chemicals, and smaller gardens mean roses must be integrated into the general planting. Today's busy lifestyles mean rose growing must be simplified and less time consuming.

The thoughts contained in this book have come from many years of growing roses, caring for other people's roses, and talking to and being influenced by other rose people. But most of all, they have come about because many years ago I fell in love with roses and the simplicity of gardening and saw no reason why the two should be mutually exclusive.

Today, after 20-plus years of growing roses, six years of running a rose care company in Los Angeles, 10 years as the owner of my former rose nursery, Ashdown Roses, and countless years of writing, talking, and spending time with gardeners, I still feel that way. And I know gardeners feel that way as well. I hope in its own way this book will teach you that you can grow roses sustainably using simple techniques and your own gardener's instincts— all applied with a healthy dose of common sense.

Mr. Allen, in closing his foreword some 60 years ago, said this: "This book is intended to strip rose culture of its complications. . . . It removes bewilderment or uncertainty and, with success, the growing of roses becomes a rich and satisfying experience."

I couldn't have said it better myself.

As you read through the book, you will see links to my *Fine Gardening* blog "Roses Are Plants, Too" (www.everydayroses.com), which contains rose how-to videos. I created these videos several years ago, because I felt that sometimes after reading how something is done, it helps to actually see it being done. Each video referenced in the book is specifically about the topic you are reading about. Read, watch, and enjoy!

Pink Drift®.

The rose Red Drift in a casual, low-maintenance planting.

Introduction:
What Is a Garden Rose?

The general perception among gardeners is that roses are fussy garden divas, and while they bear beautiful blooms, they leave little to be desired in being attractive plants. They are considered to be "sticks with flowers on top"—rigid upright growth, blooms borne only on the tops of the canes, and generally having *bare knees*, meaning there is little foliage on the bottom half of the plant. While these diva roses can be nice plants if fussed over endlessly, they will not thrive and be attractive if they are grown and treated like the other ornamental plants in your garden. Many roses sold and grown in the United States over the last 40 years fit this diva description, hence the perception that roses are hard to grow.

Garden roses are the polar opposite. At their core, they are nothing more than flowering shrubs and should be used in the garden as such. No more and no less. They live in your garden without receiving any more attention than what is given to the other shrubs.

Garden roses blend in with other plants.

Characteristics of a Garden Rose

To begin with, garden roses are naturally disease resistant. This inherent disease resistance means they do not need regular spraying programs. Instead, their own inner immune system is built up through the use of good soil, natural fertilizers, and simple care techniques—ones that work in harmony with the rose while still leaving you time on the weekend to take in a movie.

Growthwise, they have an attractive overall shape. Their growth habit is of a pleasing shape, be it rounded, tall, or gracefully arching—and this means the entire plant, not just the flower at this or that stage of bloom.

Because of this, they add to the overall aesthetic of your landscape, both in and out of flower.

Another important characteristic is that they have foliage. Don't laugh! One of the frequent comments gardeners make is that they are tired of roses that lose all their leaves due to disease or because they weren't endlessly fussed over. Garden roses are well foliated from the ground to the top. Just think of a diva rose with bare legs; it is not very useful in the garden. Imagine if the guards outside Buckingham Palace were dressed in their elegant, tall black hats and beautiful braided coats but were without any trousers. While fun for some, it would look out of place and would greatly reduce the number of people posing for photos next to them. And lastly, it is important that the leaves are healthy looking, having a nice color of green, be it light or dark.

A garden rose is above all an attractive plant, like the rose 'Oiellet Parfait' at Mottisfont Abbey in the United Kingdom.

Roses should fit the landscape.

The time it takes to breed a garden rose, evaluate it, and ultimately bring it to market takes around 10 years. From hundreds of thousands of seedlings emerge only three to five roses worthy of being released to the public, which make rose breeders heroes of the garden world. Along the way, these roses have been tested, stressed, and observed under all kinds of natural outdoor conditions. Under these testing conditions, those with the right combination of disease resistance, attractive shape, growth habit, and flower quickly make themselves known and become garden roses.

Why the Garden Rose?

Garden roses are selected for the garden differently than divas. Diva roses are generally chosen first for their flower and growth habit, and their size and health come afterward—if at all. With garden roses, the growth habit, size, and health are considered first, and the flower color and style are last. Think about it. If you want a tall flowering plant to hide the foundation of your house, would you choose pansies just because of the pretty blue flower? If you wanted a low flowering plant for the front of your flower border, would you choose camellias because of their swirled pink blooms? Of course not! It would look ridiculous.

Garden roses are selected like other plants. In other words, like other plants, they are first and foremost selected for their landscape use: What is their job in the garden? Of course the flowers are a consideration, but as with other plants, the flowers come after their landscape use. Luckily with garden roses, we are spoiled when it comes to choices of the shape and color of their flowers. Blooms on garden roses are totally an individual choice. Some gardeners love single-petal roses such as the roses Home Run®, 'Altissimo', and 'Dainty Bess'. The high, pointed centers and hybrid tea-shaped blooms have been admired by many. Some like the old-fashioned cupped blooms on antique roses, some like reflexed blooms where the petals bend out and downward, and some like the quartered blooms seen in the paintings of old masters.

With garden roses, there is a perfect choice for everyone, and everyone's choice should be appreciated. So if

the plant meets the landscape use criteria and you like the blooms, then it is a good garden rose for you. In a book on wine by Matt Kramer, he notes the question he always gets is "What is a good wine?" He responds by asking what was the most recent wine the questioner had, and did they like it? If they respond affirmatively, then he simply says, "Then for you that was a good wine." The same goes for rose flowers.

Let's be clear on one thing here: I am not applying the label "diva roses" to all roses outside of garden roses. There are many fine roses that are bred to be "cut-flower" roses, which are grown in large greenhouses to supply cut flowers for the florist industry. There are gardeners who enjoy the beauty and challenge of growing the hybrid tea roses that need more care. Additionally, there are many fine roses bred to be exhibition roses, which are grown for rose shows and shown by rose exhibitors for prizes. Each is beautiful in its own right, and rose exhibitors are some of the most talented, hardworking rose growers out there. Yet most show roses require more care and time than garden roses.

I am not saying that garden roses are better than quality exhibition or cut-flower roses. They are different from those roses because they have a different job to do. Think of a poodle. You can have one groomed to the utmost for the Westminster Kennel Club dog show, or you can have one that isn't fussed over and just romps around the backyard with the kids. Underneath it all, they are both good dogs. Like different kinds of poodles, some roses simply serve a different purpose. Exhibition roses go to the rose show, and garden roses hang out in your backyard with the family. And I'm here to tell you how to grow the roses that hang out with the family.

The Knock Out rose.

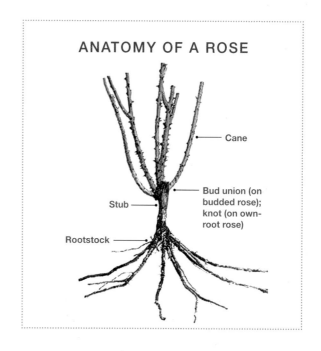

ANATOMY OF A ROSE

FACING PAGE: Select garden roses by what their job in the garden will be. Here, the rose Peach Drift adds color to the front of a plant border.

PART I

Essentials

Knock Out roses in the greenhouse at Star Roses and Plants/Conard-Pyle.

CHAPTER ONE

Buying Roses

During any given season, while there are 200 to 300 or so varieties of roses widely available in the United States via garden centers and box stores, there are closer to 7,000 actually for sale via mail order. Purchasing mail-order roses is easy, is safe, and, with a little up-front knowledge, opens the door to an incredible variety of stunning roses.

Before you buy, there are a few things you need to consider, such as how roses are sold, your budget, the season in which you want to plant, which roses do well in your climate, and what type of rose you need for how you will use it in the landscape.

You are used to buying plants by garden use; you purchase them based on criteria like color, size, and where you will plant them, with little concern for the name. Rose buying traditionally has been the opposite. Roses were bought by photo and/or name with little concern for garden use and size. You need to flip that in your mind and buy these roses as you would any other plant. Garden roses come in all shapes and sizes, and it's important to purchase the right one for the right spot.

So before you are seduced by all those beautiful photos in the catalogs and give in to an impulse buy, let's forearm you with some knowledge to help you make the best choice. And then you can get back to drooling over the pictures.

Roses range in size from small shrubs like 'Wing Ding' (top) to huge ramblers like 'Bambou' and 'Innes' (above), which grow two stories high.

Before You Buy

Let's first start with a discussion of the various ways roses are sold. There are a lot of choices, and while almost all will yield great roses, it's important to know which will work best for you. While you will have success with all of them, we'll start with the easiest.

LARGE CONTAINER

Generally, roses sold in your local garden center will come in a 3- to 5-gallon pot and occasionally a 1- or 2-gallon one. They arrive at the garden center in what is called "bud and bloom," simply meaning they have flowers to entice you into buying them.

If you are new to roses, or just an unsure gardener, this is a great way to buy roses. The garden center has already done the hard work for you by planting and nurturing the roses through their childhood. They are easy to plant and establish quickly in your garden.

DORMANT POT

Generally, these roses come in a roughly 2-gallon bio-degradable pot wrapped in plastic with a picture of the rose on it. The rose will not be leafed out or even actively

TIP: Roses in band pots should be transplanted to a larger pot and "grown on" to a more mature plant before planting in the ground. Generally, four to six months in that larger pot is sufficient.

Roses already actively growing make it easy to get off to a great start.

growing. To plant it, you simply take off the plastic and plant the whole thing—container and all—right in the ground. Over time, the pot disintegrates, and the roots get out into the soil.

These are becoming more prevalent, and they are an easy and good product to plant. If you can't plant right away, you can just leave it in the pot for up to a month. If you do, make sure to either take off the plastic or poke holes in it, so the rose drains well when you water it.

Keep in mind that you are essentially buying a rose that is just emerging from dormancy. It doesn't have a well-developed root system yet. For that reason, it will need a little more attention during the first two to three weeks in terms of watering and care than would a leafed-out, large-container plant.

TIP: If a large-container rose is not well rooted, put it back. It will lead to trouble later.

BARE ROOT

Bare-root roses are simply roses that are not sold in a pot or with soil around them. The rose arrives naked, or as they say in my part of the world, "nekkid." When they arrive, they are dormant, meaning they are not actively growing. You plant them, and then they begin to grow. They may seem a little scary at first, but once you've had success with bare-root roses—and you will—they are a cinch.

Bare-root roses have advantages, the first one being that they are much cheaper to ship through mail order, because there is no soil to add weight to the package. After all, you only need the rose. The second advantage is that they begin to immediately grow in your soil as opposed to container roses, which must first emerge from container soil before they get to the good stuff you've worked so hard to prepare (but more on that later).

The downside to bare roots is you have to plant them immediately. If you have to wait, you can keep them in a bucket of water with their roots submerged, but not for more than a few days or they will literally drown. Container roses can stay in their pots for weeks, or in some cases a few months, before you plant them.

Overall, bare-root roses are a great way to go. After you plant and succeed with the first few, your confidence level with them will go way up.

Dormant pots appear in your local garden center in spring at planting time.

Bare-root roses are a good choice for mail order.

Small-container mail-order roses are often referred to as band pots. Smaller containers are inexpensive to ship and don't take up much room in a nursery's greenhouses.

SMALL-CONTAINER MAIL ORDER

These roses range from a band pot (which is a pot that's approximately 3 inches square by 5 inches deep) to a 1-gallon pot. With today's higher shipping costs, more and more small-container roses are sold in band pots. Don't be afraid of these. Every year, thousands and thousands of rose buyers purchase band pots and have great success with them, but they take a little extra work on your part.

A band pot is a partnership between the grower and you. The grower's part is to propagate the rose and get it started to the point that it is healthy and growing. Your part is to take that young plant, transplant it from the band pot to a 1- or 2-gallon pot, spend a few months growing it to a more mature plant, and then plant it in the ground, which I go into more detail on in the planting section.

So, why buy roses in band pots? One word: selection. Earlier I said there are generally 200 to 300 varieties of roses widely available, but that being said, there are close to 7,000 roses in commerce. Guess what? Those other

TIP: Mail ordering roses offers a greater selection.

thousands of roses are generally available only from mail-order nurseries in—you guessed it—band pots!

Lastly, I'd like to touch on those roses sold in slender plastic sleeves. The sleeve is about 4 inches across and 10 inches long. It is wrapped around the plant's roots, stuffed with sawdust, and has a few rose canes sticking out of the top. Due to some manufacturers packaging them poorly, they've gotten a reputation for not being very good. Don't shy away from all of them, because when they are packaged responsibly, they can be a good bargain. The keys are knowing where to buy them and what to look for.

Only buy bagged roses from a good plant nursery or a large box store with a good garden center. They bring them in fresh and know how to take care of them. As with bare-root roses, look for green, healthy canes that are not puckered or wrinkled. If the rose has new growth coming from the canes, then up to ½ inch is acceptable. Avoid the ones in the bins at discount outlets and, yes, even drugstores. They are usually poorly packaged with hacked-off roots and are stored in less-than-ideal conditions, which dries them out, and they generally don't survive very long. There is a reason the poorly packaged ones are called "body bags"!

When to Buy Roses

Thankfully, mail-order nurseries allow you to indulge your rose-buying desires almost all year round. That being said, there are optimum times for getting the best selection.

The first thing that should drive your decision is the best time to plant for your area. Generally, this is early spring, shortly after your last average frost date, which you can find by checking with your local agricultural extension office or sometimes even by searching for it on the Internet. In the case of bare-root roses, you can go a little earlier and mound up soil or mulch to cover all but the tips of the canes to protect them until all danger of frost is past. At that point, simply pull the soil or mulch away from the canes.

Fall is also an excellent time to plant in many parts of the country, such as the South or those areas that do not get severe early frosts. As the days cool and the rose's aboveground growth begins to shut down, the soil's warmth encourages the roots to push deeper into the

Planting a newly purchased planted bare-root rose.

TIP: Watch for the fall sales. Fall is a great time for planting, and there are some bargains to be had.

Your local nurseries start to bring roses in during your area's planting time. Check with the ones you like and ask when they expect the roses to start arriving. Then be there, credit card in hand, when they do.

My purchasing schedule is this: In late fall to winter, I start looking at mail-order websites and catalogs and get my orders in for those roses. In spring, I shop my local garden centers when their roses start arriving. Lastly, in late summer, I check the mail-order sites and my local nursery for great bargains. If you follow my plan, your garden will be chockablock full of roses in no time!

How to Buy Roses

This section title may sound silly at first. Of course you know how to buy roses: You give someone money, and they give you the rose. But kidding aside, here are a few other tips for you.

KNOW YOUR GARDEN USE

As I've mentioned before—and what I'm going to keep drilling into you—first decide where you are going to plant the rose and what its use is in the landscape. Think about things like, do you need a tall rose for screening, such as the David Austin® rose 'Golden Celebration'? Or do you need some low ones for the front of a flower border, like the Easy Elegance® series of roses? Do you need a rose that will tumble over a retaining wall to soften the edges, in which case some ground-cover roses are the perfect choice? How about a low-growing rose to spread over a hillside and help with soil retention? Many of the old rambling roses and large ground-cover roses do the job with gusto. Maybe you don't like your neighbor's kids running through your backyard, so you need one that grows big and dense with long thorns to form a security

ground. Fall is also when many nurseries, both local and mail order, have their big sales, and you can really pick up some bargains. The roses may be a little root-bound or need a little cleaning up of deadwood, but if you are willing to put in a little extra work, you can save quite a bit off the old plant-buying budget—money you can use to spring for a massage after all that planting!

The best selection from mail-order websites and catalogs is generally late fall to early winter. By then, they begin to list the roses they will have for delivery the following spring. That is the time to place your order to get the best selection, but it doesn't mean you have to take delivery then. Any decent mail-order nursery will hold your roses and ship them at the correct planting time for your area. If they won't, then quickly delete their Internet address from your web browser, because they aren't worth doing business with.

TIP: Remember garden use! Make sure you are buying the right rose for the right place in your landscape design. Plant form first, flowers second.

barrier. There are a lot of roses that do that. Do you need a climbing rose to cover an old shed—one that gets large and grows vigorously like the great old rambler 'Silver Moon'—or do you need a climbing rose for the arch over your picket fence gate? The latter will need a smaller, tidier climbing rose so it doesn't snag your sweater as you bring in the groceries. Once you have figured out the type of rose you need, you are ready to part with your hard-earned money.

RESEARCH DIFFERENT STYLES

If you have access to the Internet, it is a great place to start. Browse rose websites and forums (see the Resources section on p. 178 for where to find them).

If you don't have access to the Internet, or can't get your kids off the computer long enough to use it, visit your local garden centers and by all means your local rose society and garden clubs. Bring them your list of criteria, and they can help narrow down the roses that will do best for you and your area. Bring photos of blooms that you like from books and catalogs. While those particular varieties might not work or be available, someone will likely suggest a substitute.

Whatever you do, don't get fixated on a particular variety that you've found in a lovely coffee table picture book, which was probably photographed somewhere overseas. The vast majority of roses found overseas are not available in the United States and vice versa. Just use those seductive books to figure out the color and bloom form you like. Then go "hang" that bloom on a growth habit that fits your garden use.

Before you decide where to purchase your roses, do some due diligence on the nurseries in your area. Garden clubs and local rose societies are great sources for advice on local purchases.

Starting with healthy plants is a key to success with garden roses. Here, Steve Hutton of Star Roses and Plants/Conard-Pyle plants the Pink Knock Out roses in his garden.

Easy Elegance rose Mystic Fairy®.

For container roses in bud and bloom, look for green, healthy plants without broken canes or lots of diseased leaves. Try to slip the rose out of the pot. Does it have a solid root ball that holds together, or does it fall apart? The former is good. The latter likely means the rose is still immature or that the top growth was "forced" using high-nitrogen fertilizers at the expense of the roots, which means the root system isn't big or mature enough

TIP: Research mail-order nurseries online.

Pink Drift roses.

to support all that top growth once you plant it. Put that one back and move on to the next one.

Dormant pots should have a minimum of two canes—preferably three or more. The canes should appear plump and healthy as opposed to shriveled and dehydrated. Are the cuts at the tops of the canes clean or ragged? You know which one to avoid!

With bare-root roses, look for healthy, green canes with good root systems. If the root system looks hacked, put it back. A few broken roots are OK, but only a few. Be careful of bare-root roses that are well into leafing out. They don't have the root system in place yet to support those leaves. Bud eyes swelling is OK, but avoid any with lots of foliage.

When ordering by mail, you will not be able to see the plant in person, so your due diligence will really come into play. Gardening forums and websites are terrific for checking up on mail-order nurseries (see the Resources section on p. 178). In this Internet age, if a nursery isn't good, word spreads fast. Those mail-order catalogs that

Gardener's Instincts

As you read through this book, I want you to keep one thing in mind: This is a partnership. My part is to teach you the "why-to"; in other words, to teach why you are doing something (with some how-to). Your part is to take those lessons and apply them to your garden and your own aesthetic. If I only showed how-to pruning techniques, you would just learn how to prune what works for a specific rose in a specific situation. If you learn *why* to prune, you can then apply those techniques to your own garden and roses. You may want to train a climbing rose to grow differently than what I've discussed. If you know *why* you train rose canes in a certain manner to get lots of flowers, you'll be able to free your own imagination and do just that. And I hope you do!

To do this, you are going to have to rely in part on what I call "your own gardener's instincts." These are the instincts all gardeners have that tell them when a plant is unhappy with its location or when it's struggling in the hot sun and might prefer a little shade. It's the instinct that eventually tells you that, no matter how much you try to keep a certain plant under control, it's really a thug that wants to overwhelm its neighbors, so you'd better take it out or move it. It's the little voice inside of you telling you something isn't quite right or something could be better. The "why-to" is what gives voice and confidence to those instincts.

New to gardening and don't think you have gardener's instincts? Balderdash! When you see a plant in a pot that is drooping, what do you do? You grab a watering can and water it. Did you have to read that in a book, attend a class, or research it? Of course not. You instinctively knew that plant needed water, and without thinking, you did it. When your tomato plant is falling down under the weight of summer's bright red fruit, do you leave it lying on the ground? No, you get something to hold it up. When your azaleas are performing poorly and the leaves are pale green, what do you do? You fertilize them. You instinctively know they need nourishment.

Everyone has gardener's instincts, and over time they will sharpen, just as a person learning how to cook will eventually not need to think about what herb to add. Instead, cooking instincts will signal when a dish needs a pinch of basil, and the cook does it.

Yes, as a gardener, you will make mistakes. We all do. But plants are forgiving and graciously grow back, so you can have another crack at it. I hope that by learning the "why-to," the mistakes you make won't be big—or many.

Want to know the best way to sharpen your gardener's instincts? Get away from the minutiae of "how-to" and take a moment to stop and smell the roses. And listen to what they are telling you. They know the "why-to" better than anyone.

The rose 'Silver Moon' covers a small building on the author's farm.

have a consistently good reputation for delivering healthy plants, on time, that thrive when planted, are rated high on Dave's Garden Watchdog and have a good reputation on the gardening forums.

At the end of the day, buying roses in person is going to come down to your own gardener's instincts. You know if a plant is healthy just by looking at it. The same applies to roses, so trust those instincts and enjoy your new roses!

TIP: Get your mail-order rose order in early, before they sell out. Many mail-order nurseries don't propagate in large numbers.

Buying Roses
Myth Busters

Myth: **Bigger is better when it comes to bare-root roses.** It's tempting when shopping for bare-root roses to always grab the biggest one. After all, since it's bigger at the start, won't it grow to full size that much sooner? Not always true! After a rose has been dug from the field, and before it reaches your local garden center, it has been held in "cold storage," which means it's kept just above freezing to keep it dormant. While in cold storage, it uses up stored reserves of food to live off. Then, when you plant it in the garden, it uses the reserves it has left to emerge from dormancy, grow, and wow you with flower power.

Here is the oxymoron: The larger the rose, the more energy it needs to emerge from dormancy. The smaller the rose, the less energy it uses. Therefore, a larger rose has a better chance of not having enough energy left to emerge from dormancy, because likely it doesn't have enough "gas in the tank" to make it.

So, select a nice, healthy medium-size rose instead.

Myth: **Mail-order roses from a different climate won't do well for you.** This has nothing to do with where the rose was grown. It has to do with the individual variety itself. A rose grown in a different climate may need some time to get acclimated to your area, but that has nothing to do with where it was grown. Keep in mind, this is different from a rose not liking your climate regardless of how you buy it. Some roses simply don't like certain climates, and there is nothing the gardener can do about it.

Start Shopping

Buying roses is one of the pleasures of gardening. There are so many bloom forms, colors, and growth habits that you can literally spend hours poring over catalogs and websites—a sublime way to fill up winter's bleak skies with rainbows of possibilities.

TIP: Bigger isn't always better with bare-root roses. Avoid the monsters and select a healthy medium-size plant.

Take your time, have a game plan, do your research, and trust your instincts. Doing so will ensure you get the right rose for your climate and your place in the garden. And that is a big first step toward success with garden roses!

 VIEW THE DIFFERENCE BETWEEN OWN-ROOT AND GRAFTED ROSES AT WWW.EVERYDAYROSES.COM.

The Sunny Knock Out rose.

The Differences between Own-Root and Budded Roses

The vast majority of roses sold in the United States 10 years ago were produced as what are called budded (sometimes also called grafted) roses. This is rapidly changing to the point where now more and more roses are produced as own-root roses. This very rapid shift in the way roses are produced means you as a rose buyer need to know the difference. (For more information, scan the video/QR code icon on the previous page.)

We'll begin with what is becoming a very common question these days. Should you buy own-root roses or budded roses? The answer to that question unequivocally is, buy all your garden roses as own-root roses. The "why" begins with a discussion of how they are propagated by the grower.

PREPARING ROSES

Own-root roses are produced by taking small cuttings of the rose and putting them in a rooting medium under mist until roots form from that cutting. This means the root system below the ground is the same "rose variety" as the one above the ground. Budded (or grafted) roses are propagated by taking an individual bud eye and budding it onto a rootstock. This means the rose variety below the ground is *not* the same as the one above the ground.

Both types can sprout new canes from the root system. However, with own-root roses, since the roots below the ground are the same variety as the rose above, whatever comes up from the root system is what you purchased. For this reason, own-root roses have a naturally broader base from which to produce new canes. And those canes will come from a larger area, giving you a fuller plant. In other words, a broader base equals more canes, which equals a bushier plant and more flowers. Simple, really!

A budded plant can only produce new canes from the bud union, which is that round knot above

A rose production field.

Budding roses in the production field.

the roots from which the canes emerge. When it does produce canes from the roots (or below the bud union), they are not the variety you purchased. These are called "suckers"—which does not refer to the purchaser, by the way!

WHICH IS BETTER, BUDDED OR OWN-ROOT?

There are instances when budded is better. Many exhibitor and cut flower roses do better this way. For garden roses, try to purchase own-root simply because they have that broader base from which to produce more canes and make a fuller, bushier plant.

A field of one-year-old own-root roses.

More roses are being grown as own-root roses because of the difficulty in finding skilled budders and the costs of caring for those roses. If you have never seen anyone bud roses in a field, it is back-breaking work. They bud either bent over at the waist or lying flat on carts for six to seven hours straight. Additionally, when you bud roses, you never get a 100 percent "take," which is how many sellable roses are produced by harvest time. Ninety percent is considered quite good, but in a field of, say, one million roses, that means you paid to have 100,000 roses budded that never had a "take," and that money is lost. Add in that the grower is feeding and spraying the field as a whole, and this means they are feeding and spraying roses that will never be sellable.

ESTABLISHING ROSES

One of the myths you hear about own-root roses is that they take longer to get established. This has nothing to do with own-root versus budded roses. This comes down to how old the rose was when you purchased it.

Budded roses are two years old at the time of purchase. The first year the "bud eye" emerges, and the second year the plant matures and adds more canes. Therefore, you are not buying a young plant, but in fact buying one that has a pretty mature root and cane structure.

Own-root roses are generally transplanted shortly after rooting into pots that range from a band pot to a full-size, 3-gallon pot. Generally, the roses are grown for about 6 to 10 months and then sold. This is known as "plug production," the term *plug* referring to the initial rooted small cutting before it was transplanted. So the own-root rose you purchase is approximately a year younger than a budded rose.

So, is there a middle ground between young own-root roses and mature budded ones? The answer is yes!

Field-grown own-root roses are the time-pressed gardener's dream. With this process, the plugs are simply planted directly in the ground and grown. However, since they were actively growing at planting time, they can be harvested 12 months later.

Roses grown in this manner generally appear and act similar to two-year-old field-grown budded roses. While I don't think all roses in the future will be grown this way, I do think you will see more and more of it for roses sold in large numbers. I know some growers who are switching, and in my opinion that is a good thing.

GROWING WITH SPEED

So, why do some own-root roses grow faster than others? The answer literally lies down in the soil—in the rose's roots. Since budded plants share the same rootstock, all budded roses are on equal footing—or roots. So, if you plant several budded roses of different types all at the same time, for the most part, they will all grow at a fairly similar pace. Now, I realize there is probably some rosarian reading this who can think of exceptions, and there are some, but this is a general rule, so pull in your thorns.

Own-root roses, however, are not all on equal footing. The rootstock is identical to the variety above the ground. This means one simple thing: An own-root rose will only grow as vigorously as the variety itself. Its root system is only as good as the whole plant. Therefore, the inherently vigorous variety will outpace the weaker one. Luckily, most true garden roses are of the vigorous type.

Gardening supplies at the ready.

CHAPTER TWO

Planting

Not many other points in your rose's life are more important to its survival than proper planting. This is your rose's foundation. A great deal of what you do (and don't do) when planting will ensure your garden rose's inherent inner health will be running on all cylinders. If any of you have children, you'll know how this works. Just as it's important to start a baby off with a good, nutritious diet, it is important to properly start your roses off with good soil so that there will be fewer problems later on.

The most important part of planting is creating a "living soil profile" for the entire garden bed. We are going to forget the old-school way of digging a 2-foot by 2-foot hole and only heavily amending that hole while leaving the soil around it alone and undernourished. I'll show you that, to have great roses, you should properly prepare and care for the entire bed—think whole bed, not one hole. Suffice it to say, taking the time to make sure your soil is working for you is a great first step to having carefree garden roses.

Now let's get planting!

Tools of the trade: secateurs, shovel, hooked weeding tool, and gloves.

TIP: When preparing the soil, think of the entire bed and not just the 2-foot by 2-foot planting hole.

Before You Dig

Planting may seem as simple as digging a hole, putting the plant in it, and then standing back to watch it grow. To some degree it is that simple, but you can greatly increase your chances of success by thoroughly preparing the entire garden bed beforehand. So, before you start digging, let's take a few moments to discuss what tools you may need, what to do if you are planting where roses had once grown, and, most important, how to properly prepare the entire garden bed.

TOOLS

Essentially, all you need to plant roses is a good shovel, gloves, and a pair of secateurs—the shovel to dig the hole, the gloves to protect your hands, and the secateurs to clip off broken bits of cane and/or root.

I like having two different kinds of shovels on hand. One is the standard long handle with a pointed blade, and the other is a shorter-handled one with a squared-off blade. The former roughly digs the hole, and the second squares off the sides so the rose slips in easily. As with any tools, take the time to buy a quality shovel. The specific brand doesn't matter, but when faced with several price ranges, take something from the middle price up. Nothing is more frustrating than a broken shovel on a beautiful spring planting day.

Secateurs should be the bypass variety, which means the blades pass each other when making the cut—just like scissors. You always want to use this type of secateurs for any rose chore.

The best gloves are ones thick enough to protect you from thorns but not so thick you can't use your fingers. I generally buy a nice leather pair from our local hardware store or garden center. Don't invest in expensive gloves for planting. They will be getting wet and dirty and will fall apart quickly. Save the expensive ones for pruning and grooming.

SOIL PREPARATION

You won't need any amendments at actual planting time. Proper preparation of the entire garden bed via amending well before you start planting covers all your bases. But more on that later.

You may have read or heard somewhere that you should never plant a rose in soil where roses had recently grown. The reason cited is because the new roses won't do well and may even die. This has often been referred to as "rose replant disease." There are mixed feelings about this, with some people saying it's true and some saying it isn't. We're not going to get into that debate, but there are a few things that are good to do if you plant roses in soil where some previously grew, simply because they are good ideas anyway.

The old method of dealing with rose replant disease was to remove all the old soil and replace it with fresh soil. Likely, whoever came up with this idea was able to hire someone to do it. Doing so on your own is not advisable unless you have a chiropractor on call. Another alternative was to plant something else there for a few years before you put roses back in that spot. Luckily, there is a much easier method.

Roses treated with mycorrhizal fungi do quite well in soil where roses used to be. Mycorrhizal fungi's symbiotic relationship with plants helps them take up water and nutrients, but the fungi also act as a buffer against certain harmful microbes and pathogens that may have been left behind by previous roses. By adding mycorrhizal fungi, there is no need to replace the old soil with new soil or plant something else there first.

Mycorrhizal fungi are applied by brushing them in powder form on the roots before planting, by adding the powder to the planting hole, by dipping bare-root and container roses in a liquid form, or by drenching the soil with them when you water in the newly planted rose. How you apply them will depend on whether you are planting bare-root or container roses and which method you feel is easiest. Do what works best for you.

The other key to making sure this works is understanding that mycorrhizal fungi need organic matter and nutrients to do their job. That is why the other thing to do when planting roses in an area where roses used to be is to add lots of well-rotted manure and/or compost as part of preparing the entire garden bed beforehand.

PREPARING ESTABLISHED BEDS

If you are planting in an already-established bed and can't turn over all the soil, the recipe you'll use is actually quite similar to the one mentioned in "Creating a Living Soil Profile" at right, just applied differently.

First, get one of those bulb augers you attach to a cordless drill to make holes for planting bulbs like daffodils and tulips. Drill holes 2 to 3 feet apart around the bed—

Creating a Living Soil Profile

Good preparation of the entire garden bed starts with compost. You can make your own. If you live near horse farms, you can use old, rotted manure. Or if your municipality breaks down green waste, see if they make it available to residents for free. Mushroom compost, which is the organic matter in which commercial mushrooms are grown, is also good and can be found sold in bags at your local garden center. Whatever you use, make sure it is not sterilized.

Spread the compost over the entire bed to about 2 to 4 inches. Till or fork it in. Don't beat it to death like you're making a smoothie; just work it in gently so as not to greatly disturb the existing microorganisms already hard at work. What you are adding with the compost is simply more rich food for those beneficial microbes and fungi that will help your roses take up the nutrients they need to be healthy and beautiful.

If you aren't sure about the previous history of your soil and are worried it may have become sterile, I would highly advise adding additional beneficial microbes like mycorrhiza and those that break down organic matter. There are many great organic products out there that do just that. Check with your local garden center or see the Resources section in this book (p. 178). Many are in liquid form, which you simply drench the ground with after you work in the compost. Ideally, you would do all of this a month or more before planting the bed. That time frame gives the soil a chance to settle and gives the microorganisms time to get established.

Simple arches with roses invite you down a garden path.

TIP: Create a living
soil profile to enrich
the entire bed.

no pattern needed. Drill the holes about a foot deep and pour worm castings into each hole. (Worm castings are basically worm manure. You can find them in good garden centers.) Second, pour a liquid form of beneficial microbes into each hole, about a quart per hole. Finally, put down a layer of compost and then, on top of it, put a layer of mulch. (For more information on two-layer mulching, see pp. 50–52). Keep up the two-layered mulching approach, and over time your soil will gain in health and your roses in beauty.

You can use a narrow shovel to dig the holes for the castings, but it takes a lot longer. Plus, you will end up using far more castings than you need, since the auger drills a neat, quick, and narrow hole.

When you do plant new roses in this existing bed, just dig a hole big enough to fit the plant. Mix the soil that comes out of the hole 50-50 with good, living compost. After you backfill the hole, water the rose in well with a diluted solution of the product you used to add mycorrhiza to the soil, or use the powder form to dust the hole or roots. Keep in mind that bringing an existing bed back to nature's natural rhythms doesn't happen overnight. It might take a few years, but you will see results.

Preparing your soil properly will take a little time and, yes, expense. But think of it this way: You can spend a little time and money now to lay a strong foundation so that your roses are naturally healthy, or you can spend a small fortune on chemical fertilizers and fungicides later when they struggle in poor soil. What's the cheapest way to deal with cold season, vitamin C now or a trip to the doctor later? Ditto for roses.

When and How to Plant Roses

There are two great times to plant roses: spring and fall. Spring has always been the traditional planting time because the soil is warming up and plants grow quickly and become established before the summer's heat wave comes. But an increasing number of gardening experts are also recommending fall planting.

Planting roses or any plants in fall encourages them to concentrate on building up a good root system before pushing out new top growth. In fall, as the days get shorter, plants begin to slow down their top growth. Yet the soil is still warm enough to encourage the roots to penetrate deep into the soil. Come spring, the top growth can burst forth with a large-enough root foundation to support it. For that reason, fall planting is good in all but the most extreme cold climates.

Factoring into when you should plant your roses is how you purchased them. Bare-root and dormant pot roses are generally only available in spring and therefore need to be planted right away. Fully leafed-out container plants can be planted in spring or held till fall. Mail-order band pots first need to be transplanted to a larger pot, grown on to a more mature size, and then planted—likely in fall. Additionally, as we discussed earlier, many garden centers put their roses on sale in the fall, and knowing it's OK to plant then allows you to snap up those bargains with more confidence.

If you take steps to properly prepare the soil, planting roses is really no different than planting any other plant. Simply dig a hole, and plant the roses. That being said, a few tips will help your roses out.

In "Buying Roses" (pp. 14–27), we discussed four different ways you can purchase roses, so let's discuss when and how to plant them the same four ways.

FULLY LEAFED-OUT CONTAINER PLANTS

These give the most leeway as to planting time. Most roses will live quite happily in a 3-gallon pot for up to a year. Roses sold this way start to show up in local garden centers and box stores after your last frost date in spring, and you may find them well into fall. Planting soon after purchasing is best, but if you purchase them in the heat of summer, hold off until very early fall—when the nights start to turn cool. Until that time, keep them in a spot in

The rose 'Bonica' as a tree rose.

your yard where they get afternoon shade and water them as needed. If you purchase them too late for fall planting in your climate, overwinter them in an unheated garage or shed, keeping the soil moist but not wet, and then plant them in early spring.

Start the planting process by digging a hole about 3 to 4 inches bigger than the pot. Give the pot a gentle squeeze all around to loosen it from the root ball. Don't squeeze so hard that you break up the root ball. Squeeze just enough to separate it from the pot. Examine the bottom of the pot. Are any roots coming out of the bottom weep holes? If so, use your secateurs to cut them as flush as possible with the bottom of the pot, since the roots extending out will make it difficult to remove the pot. They are likely all dried out anyway. Better to get rid of them.

Now comes the fun part: removing the rose from the pot. How successful you are with this comes down to how well rooted the rose is. Well-rooted and whole root balls will slip right out intact and tuck nicely into the hole you've dug. Here's a little tip that will help you remove the rose from the container successfully. Holding the pot upright, place your open hand over the exposed soil surface. Begin to tip the pot upside down, as if you were going to slide the root ball out. If you have small hands, you may need some help at this point. If the entire root ball starts to slide out intact, you've hit the jackpot. The rose is well rooted, and the root ball will stay intact without the walls of the pot. Slide the root ball out and lower it into the hole you've dug, and you can begin to plant. If the plant is root-bound, meaning the roots are wound tight and dense, take your clippers and score vertical lines around the root ball about 4 to 6 inches apart.

Just barely cut through the other roots. This will encourage them to grow outward from the root ball and into the soil. If you aren't sure, just make two or three vertical lines and leave it at that.

To plant the rose, first ignore the existing soil level in the pot. Just like any rose, make sure you bury the bud union (on a budded plant) or the knot (on an own-root plant) 2 to 3 inches below the soil surface in your garden. This is to prevent "wind rock," which we discuss more in the "Myth" on p. 40. Once you have your planting depth properly established by adding or taking away some soil in the bottom of the hole, begin to fill soil around the sides of the root ball. Keep tamping it in with your hands to eliminate air pockets. When the sides of the hole are half filled, pour in about a gallon of water to settle in the soil and further eliminate air pockets. When the water is gone, fill the rest of the hole with soil, and water it in well with a minimum of 2 gallons of water.

  VIEW PLANTING A GRAFTED CONTAINER ROSE AT WWW.EVERYDAYROSES.COM. *Video Note: The technique for planting an own-root container is essentially the same.*

DORMANT POT

A rose in a dormant pot can be planted right away, or you can wait and plant it slightly later. But you must plant it within one month of receiving it, at most. Keep in mind that many are sold in biodegradable pots, so make sure you plant them before the pot breaks down. As with bare-root roses, dormant pots are generally available only in spring, so you will have little choice when to plant and purchase them.

If your rose came in a biodegradable pot, plant it—pot and all—directly into the ground. The most important thing to remember—regardless of the soil level in the pot—is to bury the bud union or the knot where the canes emerge 2 to 3 inches below the soil level in your garden. Before planting, take a sharp knife or blade and score the sides of the pot to hasten the degrading process. At this point, plant it just like a fully leafed-out container rose (see pp. 33–35) and upon completion water in well.

BARE ROOT

These roses are usually only available in spring; hence, they have to be planted during that time. Additionally, since they are bare root, they need to be planted immediately. Mail-order nurseries and your local garden centers

How to Plant Fully Leafed-Out Container Roses

If your soil is well prepared, you only need a hole slightly larger than the pot.

A well-rooted rose will slide right out of the pot without the root ball falling apart.

If the rose is root-bound, use a sharp instrument to cut through the outer roots.

Use your shovel handle to make sure the rose is at the proper planting depth.

Slowly add soil, gently tamping with your hands as you go.

Always water your rose thoroughly after planting.

How to Plant Roses with a Poor Root Ball

What do you do if your rose is not well rooted and the root ball looks as if it will fall apart when taken out of the container? It's when the soil falls away—leaving you with a bare-root rose—that every gardener thinks, "Oh no, I've killed it." The danger here is that, because the rose is actively growing, having the soil fall off will tear the small white feeder roots and send the rose into shock. White feeder roots are the small, delicate roots growing off the main root system that channel water and nutrients back to the plant. When they get damaged during planting, leaves fall off, canes may droop, and, in severe cases, the plant may die.

So here is a little trick: Take a pointed or long shovel and slip it down into one side of the pot as gently as you can. Lay the pot on its side so the shovel is between the root ball and the pot wall. Thinking of the shovel as a spatula, slip the rose out of the pot using the shovel blade to support the root ball from underneath. Some soil will fall, so don't panic. Most likely, it is loose soil with no roots to hold it in place. We are interested in keeping intact that core middle of the root ball that does have new feeder roots and not harming them.

Once the root ball is out of the pot and resting on the shovel blade, carry the entire thing over to the hole. Keeping one hand on top of the root ball and with the shovel blade under it, begin to bring the root ball upright and slide it, shovel and all, into the hole. Once upright, you can gently release the shovel and let it lie against the side of the hole. It will still offer support to the root ball. Begin to fill soil in around the root ball. As you fill in more and more soil, it will support the root ball and keep that core intact. This works even better when there are two of you, one supporting the root ball and one filling in soil. When you are fully convinced the surrounding soil is supporting the root ball, slip the shovel out of the hole and continue to fill, water, and gently tamp down the soil. Don't tamp too hard or you may further break up the root ball.

In extreme cases, you can use two shovels when sliding the rose out of the pot. Place one underneath the root ball and one on top, making a "shovel sandwich." This is a very sturdy way to move a plant with a loose root ball. The planting method is the same, only this time two shovels lower it into the hole. In actuality, this method is much easier if you have to do it by yourself. You can also gently work both shovels into the pot and then cut the pot away rather than trying to slide the root ball out. Worst case scenario, if the whole thing falls apart, you can plant the rose in the hole as per the directions above, cut back half the top growth, and strip all the leaves and flowers. Doing so means the root system no longer has such a large top to support and can work to reestablish those feeder roots without the added burden of needing to supply a lot of nutrients to the part of the plant aboveground.

Finally, as with all other methods, water in well with a minimum of 2 gallons of water.

You can use a shovel to support the root ball of a plant that is not well rooted.

Use two shovels to support a rose with a very loose root ball. This is also a great way to support a rose you are transplanting.

Make sure your bare-root rose is planted deeply enough.

TIP: Roses like full sun all day, but many will do well with full morning sun. No rose likes morning shade and afternoon sun.

generally only make bare-root roses available at the optimum planting time for your area, so when they show up, it's time to plant them. If you live in a colder climate and cannot plant them when they arrive, "heel them in" by burying almost the entire plant in a trench or hole with only the tops of the canes sticking out.

When planting budded bare-root roses, first examine the actual plant. If any of the canes are broken, cut them with a sharp pair of secateurs just below the break (see "Sharpening Tools" on p. 81). Then examine the roots. Any parts broken or badly wounded? If so, snip off the damaged parts.

Dig a hole wide enough so you can fan the roots out a bit and deep enough so they don't curl back up at the bottom, generally about 12 inches wide and 18 inches deep. You've possibly read somewhere that you should make a pyramid out of the soil and lay roots over it with the base of the plant resting gently on top. Unless you are into ancient Egyptian architecture, don't bother with this.

Lower the rose into the hole while continually supporting it with one hand. You can grab it by the bud union or hold it by a cane; it doesn't matter as long as you

don't let it drop into the hole, as that could damage the roots. Making sure the bud union is around 2 to 3 inches below the soil level, use your free hand to gently start to push some soil back into the hole.

If you are planting own-root bare-root roses, you don't have a bud union, so just consider the "knot" above the roots (where all the canes come out of) to be the same as the bud union and bury it as deep.

Keep the roots fanned out a bit instead of letting them all go straight down. When the hole is about half full, give the rose a gentle shake to allow the soil to settle and eliminate air pockets. Add more soil until the hole is about two-thirds full. The rose should now be self-supporting. Stand up and gently pack the soil in with your shoe. Gently now—this isn't Irish step dancing. Pour in around 1 gallon of water and let it settle. Once the water has settled, add the rest of the soil, and then water in well with a minimum of 2 gallons of water.

  VIEW PLANTING BARE-ROOT ROSES AT WWW.EVERYDAYROSES.COM.

With any type of bare-root rose, the last chore after watering is going to be to mound up loose soil, compost, or mulch around the base of the canes to a height of about 6 inches—leaving only the top inch or so of the canes exposed. This will help prevent the exposed part of the rose from drying out until the feeder roots emerge and become established. At that point, the rose is receiving water via the root system and won't dry out. Under normal conditions, this takes about three weeks. But keep the mound there until you see the first true leaves begin to emerge. Then you know the rose has settled in and you can remove the mound. I like using mulch for the mound, because I can just spread it out in the garden bed. Don't use a dense medium like clay. This can trap in too much moisture and rot the canes. That is another reason why mulch is best.

BAND POTS

Try to arrange to have your band pots delivered in spring and transplant them to 1-gallon pots. Grow them until the root ball fills the 1-gallon pot and plant in early fall when the nights start to turn cool. If you get them late in the season and your gardener's instincts tell you that the transplanted rose has not developed a big enough root ball to fill the pot or that the top of the plant hasn't added much growth, then overwinter them in an unheated garage or shed, keeping the soil moist but not wet. Then plant in early spring.

A young rose in a band pot that's planted directly in the ground faces stiff competition from mature plants and is more vulnerable to heat, drought, wind, and so on. When transplanting it into a pot, use a good potting soil and, as with all other types of roses, ignore the existing soil level. Bury the rose about 1 inch deeper than it is in the band pot, and upon planting it in the ground, bury it another 1 inch deeper, so by the time you are done the

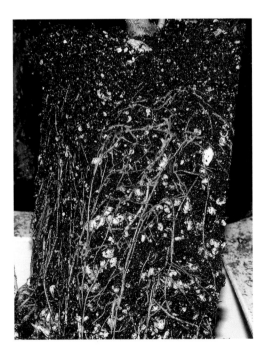

While a well-grown band pot will have a good root system, it's always a good idea to transplant roses to a larger pot and grow them bigger before planting in the ground.

TIP: Transplant band pots to a larger pot first and then plant them after the root ball is fully developed.

rose is 2 inches deeper than it was in the original pot it came in.

How long your band will take to fill the 1-gallon pot will vary widely by growing conditions and rose variety. The minimum will likely be a few months, but again your gardener's instincts are going to be the best judge. When the rose looks like it's bursting out of the pot, it's time to plant it in its permanent home in the ground. Then you can plant it just like a fully leafed-out container plant (see pp. 33–35).

  VIEW BUYING AND PLANTING OWN-ROOT ROSES AT WWW.EVERYDAYROSES.COM.

Planting in Warm Climates

If you live in an area with no winter, such as Zones 9 and 10, plant in early winter or late fall for fully leafed-out container plants. Those cooler months will allow your roses to get settled in before the summer blast furnace switches on. With bare-root and dormant pots, plant them as soon as they arrive. With band pots, it's still advisable to transplant them to 1-gallon pots and then transplant when the root ball is mature in late fall or early winter.

The beauty of the various ways roses are sold these days is the wide window for planting, with spring and fall being the best times. Worst-case scenario, no matter how you buy the roses, they all take well to being in a 3-gallon pot or larger for up to a year, which allows you even more leeway if Junior's soccer practice gets in the way.

A Few More Things to Know

Now that the rose is planted in its new home and you are dreaming of blooms to come, there are a few other things you can do to help it get off to a good start.

WATERING NEWLY PLANTED ROSES

As we discussed in "When and How to Plant Roses" (see pp. 33–38), water your rose in well with a minimum of 2 gallons of water immediately after planting. How often you water after that will greatly depend on your soil type, the weather, and whether you planted bare-root, dormant, or container roses. Because of soil type, there is no hard-and-fast rule, but there are some guidelines we can go by.

You will have to water newly planted bare-root and dormant pot roses more often while they are establishing their root system. Until bare-root roses put out and establish their white feeder roots, they will struggle to take up water, so for the first two to three weeks, water them twice as often as your other established plants. Since you cannot check under the soil to see if those white feeder roots are growing, keep up the added watering until you see actual leaves emerge on the canes. If the rose had a few leaves when you planted it, wait until new ones are actively growing. Then you can begin to slow down the watering over the next two to three weeks until you are watering on the same schedule as your other plants. During the first two weeks, you can also mist the canes once a day during the hottest part of the afternoon by squirting them from a hose. This will also raise the humidity in the air, and in this case, that is a good thing.

If you've planted an established container plant, it can be watered like most other plants in your garden. A container rose where the root ball fell apart will need more water than one where it did not, because the root system was likely damaged when that happened and needs some time to repair itself. Water these more like newly planted bare-root roses. Additionally, roses with smaller root balls generally need more water than those with large ones. Your gardener's instincts are the best guide here. Read the section on watering under "Basic Care" (see pp. 54–57) for additional watering guidelines.

TIP: Don't fertilize newly planted roses until you see the first leaves emerge.

FEEDING NEWLY PLANTED ROSES

Do not feed newly planted roses. It's best to let nature, and your living soil, run its course so the plant can get established and settled into its own rhythm. All feeding does is encourage growth the plant might not be able to sustain. When true leaves emerge from new growth, the plant is telling you it's OK to start fertilizing. For the first few months, use fertilizers that encourage root growth and not top growth. That is the middle number on the NPK scale you see on the front of most fertilizers (for more information, see "Understanding the Numbers on Fertilizer Labels" on p. 60). Avoid high nitrogen, which is the first number. There is an old saying in plants, "Bottoms first and tops second," meaning roots first and top growth second. This truly applies to roses.

PRUNING YOUNG ROSES

Don't prune newly planted roses in their first season. You can do a light trim, cut out deadwood, and do other basic chores, but don't cut them back. They need that top growth to manufacture food and grow—particularly the roots. Cutting back the tops just takes away their food factory and hinders them from quickly becoming established. Wait to prune them until after their second year.

  VIEW CARING FOR AN OWN-ROOT ROSE AT WWW.EVERYDAYROSES.COM.

Planting Myth Busters

Planting is another one of those areas where a lot of rose experts love to throw around those "must-dos" regarding how big the hole should be, how high or low the bud union should be, or what amendments should go into the hole. The list goes on, and you've likely heard or read most of them. Some make sense for certain kinds of roses, but for garden roses, most don't. And with the ever-increasing knowledge of exactly what a living soil profile is, some can actually do more harm than good. With that in mind, let's look at a few of the myths.

Myth: **You have to dig a 2-foot by 2-foot hole.** Whoever came up with this one never lived with heavy clay soil. Digging a 2-foot by 2-foot hole in that kind of hard, heavy soil involves small explosives, and we don't want to go there.

The thinking behind the 2-foot by 2-foot hole was that roses need really great soil. It's been generally discussed as the mythical goal of "sandy loam," which is the perfect balance between sand, silt, and clay. I'll buy that for fussy roses, but garden roses are not fussy. Plus, when you dig a hole in heavy soil (like clay) and replace it with new material, the roots will grow to the edge of the hole, turn, and start racing around the sides of the hole instead of penetrating into the native soil. This is called "NASCAR-ing." Additionally, disturbing the soil removes the living microorganisms that nature and we have worked so hard to build up. What is the point of building a living soil profile if you are just going to replace it with sterile soil at planting time?

When I first started growing roses some 20 years ago, I did the 2-foot by 2-foot hole. After the first year or two, I stopped and focused on properly preparing the entire garden bed before planting, and since then I have planted thousands of roses in holes no bigger than the pot they came in. And they thrive! So skip the 2-foot by 2-foot hole and focus on the entire garden bed before you plant. Your back will thank you.

Myth: **Plant budded roses with the bud union 1 to 2 inches above soil level.** Don't do this, ever! Always bury the bud union regardless of what climate you live in. Why? Two words: *wind rock*. This happens when winds come blowing through your garden and the tops of your roses start whipping back and forth. Down at the base they are also affected by the winds, and

if the bud union is too far out of the ground, they start rocking down to their roots. This loosens the soil and could tear the smaller feeder roots, impairing the plant's ability to take up nutrients and water. Additionally, air could get down there and dry the roots out. Worst-case scenario, the plant itself could completely tip over, rip out of the ground, and go from your much-loved rose to a tumbleweed.

Budded roses generally have a long stem between where the roots flare out and where the canes flare out. If you plant the bud union above the ground, then the only thing supporting that entire plant at ground level is that long stem. It's too thin and can't do it. Burying the bud union means the plant has three, five, or more canes to anchor it at soil level when those winds come howling, which prevents wind rock and potential damage to your roses.

Myth: **Put a cup of bone meal in the bottom of the hole where you will plant your roses.** The reasoning behind this is because bone meal is a phosphate, roses really need it, and since it doesn't travel through the soil quickly, it's best to put it in the hole. Some people do it and some don't, but the general thought has been *what harm can it do?* Well, let me tell you.

Recently, Linda Chalker-Scott, Ph.D., Extension Horticulturist and Associate Professor, Puyallup Research and Extension Center, Washington State University, published a paper on-line about adding bone meal to the hole when planting roses. She titled it "The Myth of Phosphate, Part II: 'Roses Need Phosphate Fertilizer for Root and Flower Growth.' " She began by noting that she could not find any scientific research saying that roses needed more phosphate than other plants. And in fact, the phosphate levels of most soils are perfectly adequate for roses and all plants. The next part is, however, very interesting.

She says: "If you add phosphate to your rose plants, you will decrease the ability of mycorrhizal fungi to colonize the rose roots. Without these fungal partners, rose roots

What to Do if a Bare-Root Rose Stops Thriving

What do you do if your bare-root rose starts to grow but then appears to be failing? Some warning signs of a failing plant are if its new growth emerges then stops, or if it even dies back. Sometimes, the tips of the canes turn black and start to die back toward the base of the plant.

This occasionally happens because bare-root roses are dug from the field long before you get them—in most cases months. They are stored in huge cold storage areas in temperatures just above freezing and kept damp. During this period, they live off the food stores they built up before they were dug from the field. The energy that remains when you plant them is needed to emerge from dormancy. If they were in cold storage too long, or didn't have enough food reserves, they struggle to emerge from dormancy when you plant them in your garden. Essentially, they start to grow but simply run out of gas before their root system can fully support them.

If this happens, immediately cut back all the canes to 2 inches high. The idea behind this is to give the roots less top growth to support with their depleted food reserves. Let the nursery you purchased the rose from know right away and even take a few photos. All good nurseries stand behind their products, but early notification is important.

Essentially, that is all there is to planting roses. There really is nothing to it if you keep in mind a few important things, the last but not least of which is to enjoy watching them grow!

An arch of roses softly shades a bench.

must work harder to extract water and nutrients from the soil." She notes that the extra phosphate is harmful to the good organisms in the soil, and she goes on to say that if you use it, the "soil health is so impacted that you must continue to add fertilizer for your plants to survive."

Now, that last statement is great news if you own stock in a chemical fertilizer company but not good news for your roses. Those living soil organisms supply the natural nutrients that work in harmony with your roses to boost

their own natural immune system. Professor Chalker-Scott is suggesting that by adding artificial fertilizers, we are actually getting in the way of that process. She goes on to say: "I believe this is what has happened in many landscapes that feature roses. Well-intentioned, yet misguided, homeowners overapply phosphate and other fertilizers, insecticides, and fungicides until the soil system is so impacted that it becomes non-functional." So I say, let's skip the bone meal, shall we?

Myth: When planting roses, keep them far enough apart to allow for lots of "air circulation." The response to this one when asked "why" is that this will help prevent disease. To which the response should be, "Why are you planting disease-prone roses in the first place?"

This idea also came about from the early rose exhibitors who needed to get around their roses to groom them for show. Plus, they logically didn't want the flowers bumping into each other and causing damage, which makes perfect sense if you exhibit.

With garden roses, there is no need for lots of air circulation if you aren't exhibiting them. More important, they are disease resistant by nature. Using USDA Hardiness Zones 6 and 7 as the average, most garden roses in those zones can be planted 20 to 30 inches apart, depend-

The rose 'Dortmund' thriving in dappled light under trees.

Plant garden roses close enough so they gently grow into each other. 'Roseraie de l'Haÿ' just south of Paris.

ing on how big the bush ultimately gets and where you live. In warmer climates, space them a little farther, and in colder ones, tighten that up a bit. Like all plants in the garden, roses should be allowed to grow into each other so instead of seeing brown mulch between them, you see a floating carpet of blooms from one end to the other. Let the roses greet by "shaking blooms" with each other, like you would in a classic flower border. Yes, as with any time you plant something, be careful of overcrowding and use your instincts to properly space your roses for design, but don't worry about lots of air circulation. If someone rants about it, suggest they buy a few giant fans.

Myth: Roses can't grow in shade. There is truth to this one. No rose will thrive in total shade. Many can take half a day of sun as long as it is morning sun. Dark red roses actually hold their color better when exposed to morning sun and then shade from the hot afternoon's rays. Full sun for roses is a minimum of six hours—as long as it's morning sun. No rose will be happy in morning shade and only afternoon sun. Some rose classes like Hybrid Musks and polyanthas can take

dappled sunlight and do well under high canopies of light hardwood trees.

Here is another good rule of thumb: The fewer petals a rose has, the better it will do with lower sunlight. Fewer petals means the bloom doesn't need as much sun to dry off the morning dew.

Ideally, however, all roses prefer full sun from morning to night. Those conditions will always get the best from your roses unless you live in the desert, where they will appreciate a little afternoon shade!

  VIEW PLANTING A ROSE IN LESS SUNLIGHT AT WWW.EVERYDAYROSES.COM.

Myth: Always water in with vitamin B1 right after planting. Vitamin B1 supposedly helps with transplant shock, hence the recommendation. While this appears to do no harm, roses have been planted without it and have done just fine. Frankly, proper planting is the best way to prevent shock, and a part of this is good old plain water. But if you wish to use B1, by all means go ahead.

What Is a Living Profile?

If it's true a house is only as good as its foundation, then a garden is only as good as its soil. A soil full of life such as microbes and beneficial fungi is as old as nature itself. Think of a forest floor that is undisturbed. Everyone agrees it is a rich soil environment because over the years, leaves and limbs fall and decompose into the soil every season. Plus no one comes through and disturbs it by rototilling, thereby upsetting the life in the soil. This is known as a living soil profile. The soil is alive with microbes and beneficial fungi working in harmony with the plants to help them grow and be healthy.

WHY CREATE ONE?

More and more studies, articles, and talks are highlighting the symbiotic relationship between plant life and the soil's microorganisms, the most widely discussed being mycorrhiza. Knowing what they do and how they work will help you better understand why preparing the entire bed is paramount.

A simple explanation is this: Mycorrhiza are naturally occurring beneficial fungi that attach themselves to the roots of the plant. They put out tendrils that can go well into the soil—far beyond the reach of the plant's roots. They channel water and nutrients back to the plant and in exchange receive sugars such as glucose and sucrose from the plant.

Roses, perennials, and annuals thrive in close proximity.

Because the plant's reach is now well beyond its root system, it can better withstand drought, bring in more minerals and nutrients, and thereby enhance its own inner immune system. Simply put, you will have healthier roses that are better able to naturally withstand whatever nature throws their way. This is known as using "probiotics"—proactively using nature to help your plants.

If we never disturbed our soil, Mother Nature would take care of this for us. But as we prepare garden beds, plant new plants, and clean out old debris, we interfere with that process—not because we are bad gardeners, but because we like to plant things!

HOW DO I CREATE ONE?

Achieving this living soil profile in the entire bed before planting is actually quite simple. In fact, nature started working on it for you a few million years ago! Unless you have been constantly spraying your soil with fungicides and chemicals, the mycorrhiza are already there. You can enhance them with compost that you spread over the entire bed to about 2 to 4 inches. Then till or fork it in. What you are adding with the compost is simply more rich food for those beneficial microbes and fungi and through them, your roses. If you think your soil is sterile, you can add additional mycorrhiza, which can be bought from your local garden center. If you are planting in an already-established bed and can't turn over the entire soil, find a product that will add mycorrhiza to the soil and apply it to your entire bed.

It's amazing how a little compost can get the soil's microbes working again. When I ran my rose care company in Los Angeles, the first thing we did when we took on a new client was to go to the Los Angeles Equestrian Center and purchase truckloads of composted manure. We would spread it over the entire rose bed, add fresh mulch on top, and within months we'd have new growth, larger and more blooms, and happy customers. We looked like geniuses, when in fact all we did was give nature a helping hand. Well, we and the horses!

A living soil profile (above) means you don't have to use lots of amendments at planting time, which results in naturally healthier plants (right).

PART 2

Basic Care

Watering a newly planted rose.

CHAPTER THREE

Mulching, Watering, and Feeding

Did you know that plants have immune systems much like humans? The recent trend toward environmentally friendly plant care methods and products is creating a greater understanding of how a plant uses soil, microorganisms, and water to boost its own immune system. Since garden roses are bred to be disease resistant, they arrive in your garden with already strong immune systems. Our job is to enhance this with good nutrition, not replace it with chemicals.

Because we've recently developed a greater understanding of natural plant care, we have learned better ways to care for our roses. For example, we now know that mulching is a key component of a rose's ability to withstand the whims of Mother Nature. Too much watering hurts your rose's chance of surviving a drought. Overfeeding with quick-release products isn't good for garden roses. And traditional pests, like aphids, are actually an important part of the cycle when it comes to attracting beneficial insects. The care methods I talk about are all part of a complete and interrelated approach to helping your roses be at their best. Feeding is part of preventing disease, mulching is part of feeding, and not using pesticides is part of pest prevention.

Along with this new way of thinking comes the realization that not all in nature is perfect or should be.

Mulch keeps weeds down, keeps the soil temperature consistent, and helps retain water. And it looks good!

Mulching

Proper mulching is a very important part of rose care. Mulch feeds the soil by breaking down into the compost needed to feed the beneficial microbes. It keeps the root zone cool by protecting the soil from the sun's hot rays. It keeps weeds down by shading out the sunlight they need to germinate, and it retains moisture in the soil, all of which add to the natural health of your roses.

Before You Mulch

First, it's important to have a basic understanding of what mulch is, what compost is, and why the two-layered mulch approach is the best way to go.

Mulch is basically fresh material you put over the soil for the reasons mentioned above. In most cases, it's either fresh hardwood mulch made from hardwood trees, fresh

pine mulch from pine trees, or fresh pine needles (sometimes called pine straw).

Compost is organic material after it has been broken down. In fact, mulch (fresh materials) over time becomes compost. That's an important thing to note, and why it is will become clear in a moment.

Second, let's talk about why it's important to properly apply mulch. Fresh mulch needs nitrogen to break down. It pulls nitrogen from the air and from the soil beneath it. Therefore, if you put fresh mulch on bare ground, it actually pulls nitrogen from the soil, thereby robbing your plants of the nitrogen they need. The same thing happens if you remove all the old mulch first and then put fresh mulch down on the bare ground.

However, once the mulch is broken down into compost, the reverse happens. It begins to emit nitrogen down into the soil and into the air.

That is why the first layer should always be compost. It is your nitrogen-emitting layer. It emits nitrogen in two directions: first, to the ground, and second, into the fresh layer of mulch you put on top of it, thereby helping it break down. This means your fresh mulch is no longer taking nitrogen from your plants as it breaks down. The compost is acting as a nitrogen-emitting buffer between your plants and the fresh mulch.

Finally, let's discuss what we are trying to achieve. We previously mentioned that a forest floor is one of the richest soil environments in the world, and we want to duplicate that in our garden. It's rich because every autumn, all the leaves fall and, over the next year, rot into the soil and become compost. The fresh leaves (read "mulch") that fall this year lie on top of a nitrogen-buffering compost layer made of—you guessed it—last year's leaves, which by now have broken down into compost. Over the next 12 months, this year's fresh leaves break down, and next year they become the compost layer. This process simply repeats itself year in and year out. And that's what we want in our gardens.

THE TWO-LAYER APPROACH

This is where the two-layered mulch approach comes in. It does nothing more than replicate what Mother Nature has been doing for the forest floor for millions of years, which is to have "fresh mulch" fall from the trees in autumn and become compost over the next year, and then to have that process repeat itself the following year and beyond.

When recreating this process in your own garden, remember two quick notes: First, don't use nondegradable materials like stone for mulch. They will not break down into the compost your soil needs to stay alive.

Second, use freshly ground hardwood as mulch instead of pine or pine needles. The best hardwood mulch is double ground, sometimes also called double hammered, which means it's been ground twice to help jump-start the composting process. Pine needles can make the soil more acidic over time, and roses like a neutral pH. The exception, of course, is if you live in an area with a soil high in pH (like the alkaline soil found in some western states). Additionally, there is some evidence emerging that mulch from hardwoods native to your area may aid in disease suppression.

Try to avoid bagged mulches. First, you don't know what kind of wood is in there. Second, it may not have a lot of the beneficial microbes needed to break it down.

TIP: Bring the forest floor to your backyard by using mulch.

Good soil equals healthy plants.

The Double Knock Out rose.

notice your mulch getting a little thin during the season, never be afraid to add more at any time.

The two-layered mulch approach is quite simple. It involves a layer of compost covered by a layer of fresh mulch, and each year, like our forest floor, this is renewed.

If you have never used the two-layered mulch approach (meaning you only used fresh mulch on bare ground or always removed the old mulch), you will have to jump-start the process. To do this, use actual compost first. Then put fresh mulch on top. Repeat this for the first two to three years. After that, the fresh hardwood mulch will be breaking down quickly enough over a season to become the compost layer the following season, and that is why it's important to know that fresh mulch becomes compost over time. Subsequently, all you need to do is keep adding fresh hardwood mulch on top of last year's mulch, which has by now become the compost layer. But before you add the fresh mulch, use a garden fork to gently turn the old mulch into the top 1 to 2 inches of the soil. And that is what the two-layered mulch approach is all about!

Some seasons may require more compost beneath the fresh hardwood if you feel that the bottom layer is thin, but generally, by the time the whole thing gets "cooking," additional compost is no longer needed—just fresh hardwood as necessary. Keep repeating this process, and within a few years, your soil will be alive, holes will be easy to dig, the roses will be happy, and new ones will spring to life almost as soon as their roots hit the hole.

TIP: Use the two-layered mulch approach.

When and How to Mulch

It's best to mulch when it's easiest, and with roses, that is right after you prune. Since the roses are cut back, it's simpler to get in and out of the planting bed without getting torn up from their thorns. This being said, if you

A Few More Points about Mulching

If you think the fresh mulch is not breaking down but instead is becoming "matted," meaning it is tightly knit together and not allowing water and air to penetrate it, then you need to jump-start the composting process. To begin, take out the old mulch that has not broken down. Next, put down a layer of fresh compost that you are sure is aged. Then put a fresh layer of hardwood mulch over that.

Finally, we are going to address the reason the previous layer of mulch did not break down. We are going to add beneficial soil microbes through a soil inoculant. There

TIP: Don't rake out the old mulch. It's the compost layer!

are essentially two groups of microbes needed to break down mulch and begin composting. The first kind breaks down the fresh mulch, including some microbes that actually shred the mulch. The second kind then breaks the mulch down even further and eventually converts the resulting compost to soil.

The product used for this is a liquid microbial soil inoculant, and it is applied as a drench right over the freshly laid compost and mulch layer. When looking at the label on the product, there are two things to look for.

First, it should have a high diversity of microbial varieties. As an example, the product I helped develop, Biltmore Naturals™ Rose Boost, has more than 40. That is a good benchmark.

Second, it should have a high CFU count per ounce. CFU stands for colony forming units, and it is the way viable cells are measured in microbiology. Biltmore Natural Rose Boost has more than 13.89 million CFUs per ounce. Some products only have 26,000 CFUs per ounce.

Mulching Myth Busters

Myth: Always remove the old mulch first before you add new mulch. The thought behind this was that disease spores like black spot and powdery mildew could overwinter in the mulch. If your mulch is actively breaking down every year (composting), disease spores will not live over the winter. The composting action will break them down, much like it does weed seeds. However, as previously mentioned, if the mulch is not breaking down, then take it out and restart the process.

Myth: If I keep adding fresh mulch, my garden's soil level will get higher and higher, eventually burying the plants. Not if you have properly created and maintained that living soil profile we talked about previously. All those beneficial microbes will "eat" all that good compost, and it will simply disappear in the soil as they do their job.

Still not convinced? Think of those majestic redwood trees that are 2,000 years old. If every year the soil in the forest where they live got higher and higher, they'd be pretty short by now!

Proper care encourages young roses and rose growers.

Roses frame a bridge at Mottisfont Abbey in the United Kingdom.

Watering

All plants like water, and roses are no exception. The best source of water is nature's own rainfall, and in many parts of the country, roses don't need anything else. Additionally, when properly planted, cared for, and watered, roses can go a few weeks between showers. During droughts, my mature roses have gone as long as a month with no water and suffered little from it.

But if you must water, keep this one simple rule in mind: Roses like infrequent, deep watering. They do not like to be watered a little every day. Rather, they like to get a good soaking, then be allowed to dry out, and then get soaked deeply again.

Before You Water

How often roses need water varies widely due to climate, soil types, and the maturity of the roses.

If you have clay soil or live in a cooler climate, you may find you need to water less frequently. In that case, water-

TIP: Roses like infrequent, deep watering.

ing with a garden hose may be best. If you'd like, you can use an oscillating sprinkler on the end of a hose, since on hot days roses love a good bath.

If you have a sprinkler system that waters your lawn, make sure it is not accidentally watering the roses as well. Lawns need a lot more water than roses do, and if the sprinklers for your lawn are also watering your rose beds, that will be too much water for them. Additionally, you tend to water your lawn far more frequently than roses like, and this can cause the roses to have yellowing leaves, make them more susceptible to disease, and even kill them.

If you live in a dry climate or in an area with sandy soil that drains quickly, you may need to water quite frequently. In that case, you may choose to install permanent irrigation. A system that covers the entire bed with water is a better choice than individual bubblers. With the latter, every time you add or move a rose, you need to add a bubbler. Plus, just as I discussed in planting, you need to think of the entire bed when it comes to watering. For that reason, soaker lines beneath the mulch work well. Just make sure you know where your soaker lines are before you start digging holes for new roses!

Speak to an irrigation expert and tell him you would like the entire bed covered in a way that allows infrequent, deep watering. He will be able to pick the right system for your needs.

When and How to Water

While there is no hard-and-fast rule on how often you should water, there is a way to let your roses tell you. First, give your roses a good, deep watering, either by rainfall or irrigation. Note the day you did it on your calendar. Then start watching the roses. When the leaves start to droop, you've gone one day too long. Note that date and count back the number of days to when you first watered. Subtract one day, and that is how often you should be watering. Keep in mind that when temperatures exceed 90°F, the leaves may naturally wilt due to heat. But don't confuse wilt from heat with wilt from underwatering.

Try this at different times of the year, as seasons determine how often you should water. Additionally, as your roses mature, their roots go deeper, and your living soil profile matures, you will need to water less often. Finally, infrequent watering encourages the roses to push their roots out and down to increase the area in which they can find water on their own.

How can you tell if you are over- or underwatering? The symptoms of each often look the same from a distance: droopy leaves. But you can tell the difference by feeling the leaves. If they are soggy, they've gotten too much water. If they lean toward crispy, it's time to increase the watering.

If you have an irrigation system, monitor the irrigation clock and be ready to adjust the water schedule at various times of the year, and particularly during rainy spells. A rainfall followed by a scheduled watering a day later often leads to trouble.

Watering Myth Busters

Myth: **Roses need lots of water.** They actually don't. The key is to let them get their roots deep into the ground. That is achieved by infrequent, deep watering plus watering the entire area and not just around the roses. This forces the rose to send its roots out looking for moisture. Mycorrhiza play an important part in this in the living soil profile. This is why it is important to water your roses to get them established, and then encour-

Watering the Peach Drift roses.

Here, the Pink Knock Out rose complements the landscape.

TIP: Overwatering weakens roses, making them more susceptible to disease.

age them to fend for themselves with the help of those beneficial microbes.

Myth: **Don't water overhead.** My standard response to this one is, "What do you do when it's raining? Go stand out there with an umbrella?" Overhead watering cleans the leaves, and if done early enough in the day (so the leaves dry out well before the sun goes down), it actually helps in disease suppression. Most disease spores take up to 24 hours to attach themselves to the

Roses and clematis are very traditional plant companions. The rose 'Königin von Dänemark.'

TIP: Water the whole bed, not just each individual rose.

leaves. You can sometimes wash them off with overhead water before they have a chance to develop. So it's OK to grab a hose and give your roses a bath on hot, dry days. They love it!

Myth: The hotter it gets, the more you should water. No. Roses actually shut down in the heat as part of their natural rhythm. During hot weather roses frequently require less water, and it's best to let them naturally go semi-dormant. Increasing the water keeps them from going dormant. When they are actively growing and blooming, in spring and late summer/early fall, is when they need lots of water.

 VIDEO: VIEW SUMMER CARE TIPS FOR YOUR ROSES AT WWW.EVERYDAYROSES.COM.

Feeding

There is a great deal of information out there when it comes to fertilizing roses—almost as much as there are actual products to feed them with. The sheer number of feeding programs can make feeding roses seem overly complicated. What you want to get out of your roses determines how you feed them.

If you exhibit roses, you will need a pretty intensive feeding program to produce a "Queen of Show" bloom. Some of these programs involve applying all kinds of different products on a weekly basis, leaving you little time to stop and smell the roses. There is nothing wrong with that if you exhibit. It takes that kind of hard work and dedication to pull in the prizes. But for the average gardener growing garden roses, those programs are overkill. Additionally, garden roses don't like heavy feeding. When overfed, they tend to throw off lots of green growth at the expense of the blooms. So is there a simple way to fertilize your roses without having to give up your all your spare time? Thankfully, there is. Stay tuned!

Roses thrive in the loving soil at Mottisfont Abbey.

A Simple Three-Part Feeding Program

Part 1: Apply an organic time-release fertilizer in early spring and another in late summer based on the times discussed in "When to Start and Stop Feeding Roses" (see pp. 60–61).

Part 2: Take proper care of your soil. Most everything your roses need to be healthy is in your soil, and it's our job to make sure it is available to them, which comes from creating a living soil profile at planting time (see p. 31). Then, incorporate the two-layered approach to mulching on a regular basis (see pp. 50–51).

Part 3: Use a seaweed-based fertilizer. How often you apply it can depend on the particular kind, but as long as you are doing parts 1 and 2, once a month is plenty. You can actually do without it and just do parts 1 and 2, but if you don't mind a little extra work, you will be pleased with the results.

Before Feeding Your Roses

As previously discussed, a living soil profile plays a major role in feeding your roses. That living soil contains many of the nutrients your roses need already. Plus, those microbes are great at helping to get those nutrients to your roses. If, like the forest floor, our garden was thousands of years old, all the needed nutrients would be there, having built up over time. However, since our gardens are not nearly that old, our goal with a fertilizer is simply to make sure all the nutrients needed are steadily delivered into the soil so the microbes can help deliver them to your roses.

For this reason, time-release granular organics are the best. These fertilizers put out natural nutrients into the soil at a slow pace over several months. Garden roses prefer that kind of slow, lazy feeding during the season—as do many gardeners!

FEEDING FREQUENCY

You should fertilize two times during the season. The first is in early spring, and it should be with a well-balanced, long-term, time-release fertilizer that will last up to four months. In late summer, you should use a short-term fertilizer that will last about two months and have less nitrogen, which is the first number on the NPK scale (see "Understanding the Numbers on Fertilizer Labels" on p. 60). Nitrogen stimulates new growth, which is something you don't want going into winter because it could be harmed by an early freeze. Since many time-release fertilizers actually shut down when soil temperatures drop, you can play with this a little. Check the label of whatever you buy for more detailed information. Or ask your local garden center to see what they recommend.

For a foliar feed, which is applying a liquid fertilizer to the leaves, use a seaweed-based spray. Liquid seaweed-based fertilizers do wonders when applied as a foliar spray. The foliage turns a darker green, the colors on the blooms become more intense, and the canes are hardier. Overall, the plants are happier. Liquid seaweed is rich in potassium, minerals, and trace elements, and they even contain some growth hormones. It's also very good at making these nutrients available to the plant. The other advantage to using seaweed is that, when used as a foliar spray, it also helps in disease resistance; it builds up the

The Double Knock Out and Pink Knock Out, when closely planted, provide a carpet of flowers.

foliage in a way that makes it more resistant to pathogens such as black spot and mildew. As with the organic granular, if our "forest floor" was thousands of years old, we likely wouldn't need this, but since it's not, a little harmonious assistance is good.

CHEMICAL FERTILIZERS

Let's take a moment to discuss chemical (or synthetic) fertilizers. They are not all bad. Some of the synthetic

TIP: Feed using organics. They feed the soil—not just the roses.

time-release fertilizers do work, and the liquids can be good for a short burst if you need to get your roses in tip-top shape quickly for that upcoming garden party or backyard wedding. If you have some in your garden shed, by all means use them up. No point in throwing them away and wasting valuable gardening funds that could be better spent on buying roses. But once they are gone, make a switch to organic-based time-release fertilizers. The good ones have the added advantage of also feeding the soil at the same time—kind of a two-for-one.

This brings us to those all-in-one fertilizer, insect control, and disease control products. Generally granular, they are applied by sprinkling the granules around the base of each rose. Essentially, they work by putting the chemical fungicide and insecticide in the soil, where they are taken up by the rose's roots, are absorbed into the plant, and then fight insects and disease from within the plant. While I am not saying these products don't work—because they do—you can run the risk of harming the beneficial fungi like mycorrhiza that have colonized around the roots. That can run contrary to our overall goal of creating a living soil profile.

When to Start and Stop Feeding Roses

When to start and stop feeding roses will, of course, vary widely by where you live, but here are a few rules of thumb.

If you live in a climate with a true winter, you do not want to be feeding your roses during a time of year when a freeze can happen. For this reason, be careful of feeding too early in spring or too late in fall. To know when to start feeding your roses in early spring, you need to figure out the last frost date (Marker 1) for your area and listen to your roses. If your average last frost date is in early April, the soonest you want to start feeding is 30 days before that, or in early March. The other thing to look for is if, 30 days before your last frost date, your roses have put out their first growth and initial true sets of leaves (Marker 2), go ahead and start feeding. If not, wait until they do so.

However, if you get a warm spell midwinter and the roses put out some leaves 60 or even 90 days before your last frost date, don't start feeding! Wait until the 30-day

Marker 1 regardless of what the roses are doing. Nature is fickle, and we've all had that warm spell in January followed by a blast of winter in February.

To review when to start: Marker 1 is 30 days before your last frost date in spring. Marker 2 is when your roses have put out some leaves after Marker 1 has passed.

Understanding the Numbers on Fertilizer Labels

Almost all fertilizers have three numbers on the label. They may be 10-10-10 or 12-8-6. But what do they mean? These numbers are known as the NPK scale. Simply put, each number represents the percentage of the three major nutrients that are present in fertilizers. They always appear in the same order: N = nitrogen, P = phosphorus, K = potassium.

Each one has a different function. (N) Nitrogen provides plants with the ability to produce more chlorophyll, which allows them to grow more quickly. (P) Phosphorus aids in root development. (K) Potassium helps the transport of nutrients through the plant, which helps fight disease, aids in drought and cold tolerance, and also increases flowering ability and size of blooms.

Good-quality organic fertilizers are nicely balanced, but the number to keep in mind is the first one, the nitrogen number—it should be higher in spring and lower in fall so you are not pushing new growth into winter. The last number, potassium, should be the opposite— lower in spring and higher in fall because it helps plants withstand winter.

Rose hips are the bright orange berries that form in winter. Besides being a spot of color, they are a great food source for birds.

To know when to put your last feeding down, watch the weather at the end of summer. Summer is defined as generally warm days and, more important for this conversation, warm nights. But when the nights turn cool, the plants start actively growing again. You can actually see the fresh bronze-tipped leaves emerging on your roses. That is when to put down the last granular feeding. For liquid fertilizers, start after the last frost date in spring and end about 30 days before your first frost date in fall. If you aren't sure of your frost dates, contact your local agricultural agent or (as I did in my case) Google it.

If you live in an area with no true winter, you are safe to feed at most any time as the roses need it. Keep in mind that in hot climates, summer is actually the rose's dormant season, so use a light hand during that time. Again, let the roses tell you. If they are no longer putting out new growth, then they are going to bed, so let them. I imagine you wouldn't want to put your head on the pillow at 11 p.m., only to be awakened an hour later by someone trying to force a hamburger down your throat. Ditto for your roses.

Feeding Roses Myth Busters

Myth: Roses need a lot of fertilizer. Exhibition and florist roses need lots of food. Garden roses do not. Since they are vigorous by nature, a feeding program designed to enhance what they naturally do on their own is all they need.

Myth: You need to rotate several different fertilizers. If you exhibit, yes. If you just want nice garden roses in your landscape with nice foliage and flowers, you do not. Just use the method described in "A Simple Three-Part Feeding Program," p. 58.

Putting It All Together

The key thing to take away after reading this is that mulching, watering, and feeding are all interrelated. Mulching is part of feeding because it keeps the living soil profile alive. Watering also contributes to the living soil profile, and proper watering better enables the roses to withstand drought and cold. Good organic fertilizers not only feed the plants, but they also provide nutrients to those beneficial microbes we've worked so hard to build up with mulching.

All of these together contribute to our overall goal of boosting our roses' own inner immune system, giving us healthier, happier, and more beautiful roses.

TIP: Less is more with garden roses. Overfeeding leads to green growth at the expense of blooms.

What Is an International Style Rose Trial?

An International Style Rose Trial is one that judges the entire rose plant (not just the flower) over a two-year period. The purpose is to test roses in public gardens using methods similar to what a home gardener may use. During the two years, the roses are judged in areas such as growth habit, buds and flowers, disease resistance, recurrent flowering, and fragrance.

While there is no hard-and-fast set of rules that all trials go by, all the international trials use similar guidelines. To keep the testing to newer varieties, they limit how long a rose has been available to buy. It can vary anywhere from no more than five years in the market to never having been sold at all. The entrant must supply several bushes of the same variety. They are all planted together, so the judges are not just looking at one bush per variety but a grouped planting.

Unlike some industry trials that are entered by nurseries, International Style Rose Trials are entered by the rose breeders themselves. This means they are much more accessible to all rose breeders—from amateur to professional. William Radler, who bred Knock Out roses, was an amateur rose breeder when the variety first came to market!

HOW ROSES ARE SCORED

To make sure the entire bush is scored (and not just the flower), the judges' scoring sheet notes specific attributes that add up to the overall score. Again, they can vary slightly from trial to trial, but an example might be:

- Growth habit and vigor: 25 percent of overall score
- Buds and flowers: 20 percent of overall score
- Recurrent bloom: 20 percent of overall score
- Resistance to disease: 25 percent of overall score
- Fragrance: 10 percent of overall score

A permanent panel of judges scores the entries three to four times a year over the trial period. At the end of the trial, an international jury comes in and scores them one time. That same day, an awards banquet is held and the top roses are revealed.

The roses are grouped into classes with a winner from each class, such as Ground cover, Hybrid Tea, Floribunda, Shrub, and Climber. Other awards classes that focus on a particular attribute, such as fragrance and disease resistance, are often included.

The top prize for the trial goes to the rose that has the highest score among all of them. This award is frequently called the Golden Award. The winner of this award has bragging rights until the next year's ceremony!

Up until recently, most of these trials were in Europe in cities such as The Hague, Paris, Lyon, Monza (Italy), Rome, Baden-Baden (Germany), and the like. Luckily, there are now two in America. The first took place in Rose Hills in southern California, and the second is taking place at the Biltmore International Rose Trials in Asheville, North Carolina.

International jury at The Bagatelle Trials in Paris.

ABOVE: The historic walled rose garden at Biltmore.

BELOW: The Biltmore International Rose Trials also allow the public to vote for their favorite rose.

BILTMORE ROSE TRIALS

The Biltmore International Rose Trials began in 2011 and are being conducted on the grounds of the Biltmore Estate. They take place in the walled rose ground just off the main house—a truly stunning setting for such a trial. There, the public can get in on the act. In front of each trial rose there is sign explaining how anyone can vote for roses they like by texting in their vote. The rose with the most votes will win the Biltmore Guest Choice Award at the end of the two-year trial period.

The Biltmore International Rose Trials are a non-chemical rose trial. Instead, they use environmentally friendly products much in the way you would use them in your garden.

It's important that the rose-buying public understand what is behind the various kinds of trials. This way, when you see a rose advertised as having won an award from one of them, you will know if that rose was tested similarly to how you will grow it in your own garden.

International Rose Trials

Please vote for your favorite rose so we can determine the "Biltmore Rose Guest Choice Award."

The roses in this bed are part of a two-year trial during which our gardeners and international judges will evaluate the plants for garden performance, fragrance, and disease resistance.

Texting instructions are provided at each rose in the trial. Thank you for your assistance!

Green lacewing and a ladybug resting on a rose.

CHAPTER FOUR

Disease and Insects

Would you take antibiotics 365 days a year because you think someday you may catch a cold? Of course not, and if it sounds preposterous, then think of this: Spraying roses weekly with chemical fungicides even when they don't have disease is the same thing as taking antibiotics every day even if you aren't sick. Regularly spraying chemical insecticides on plants regardless of whether there is an infestation kills the good bugs (beneficial insects) in your garden that eat the bad guys.

While both examples are extreme, sadly, they express the "theory" behind the use of many chemical disease and insect treatments for your garden. We are encouraged to constantly use those chemicals even when there is nothing wrong or nothing to treat.

Instead of taking antibiotics for a cold that doesn't exist, wouldn't it be better to boost your immune system so when cold season comes around, your body is ready to fight it off on its own?

That's what this chapter is about, and it illustrates how we are going to approach the issues of disease and insects—through prevention. By properly selecting, caring, and feeding a rose variety, you will have little trouble with disease during the season. And by learning about the relationship between the good insects and the bad ones, you can learn how to keep the good ones around and ready to do their job. Be proactive by giving nature a helping hand!

Disease

Did you know there are beneficial fungi that fight disease just as there are beneficial insects that fight bad insects? There are, and encouraging these beneficial fungi is the best thing you can do to fight disease. Think of them as the plants' white blood cells, ready to tackle anything that threatens to infect your roses. Strengthening them through nutrition is the best line of defense against disease.

While some books like to list every disease a rose—or any plant—can possibly get, we are going to keep this to the most common ones found on landscape roses. They are black spot, powdery mildew, rust, and downy mildew.

Garden roses are bred to be disease resistant. If you start with good nutrition, your garden rose will be equipped to handle fighting off disease on its own, but if needed, you can briefly intervene. I keep it simple, and deal with all four diseases in a like manner, so there is no need to have a shed full of different products for each disease. As for tools, if you need to spray, all you will need is a 1- or 2-gallon pump sprayer or a hose-end sprayer.

The Most Common Diseases

I won't go into a long scientific thesis on how the following diseases are caused because, frankly, I suspect you don't care. For our purposes, just know they are caused by airborne spores that appear and multiply under the right kind of weather conditions. You just want to be able to identify and deal with them. So let me tell you how to do that.

BLACK SPOT
This is perhaps the most common one. It's a fungal infection. You know your roses have it when you start to see random black spots on the top of their leaves. The leaves will progressively turn yellow and start to fall off. The time to be on the lookout is during warm, humid conditions.

POWDERY MILDEW
Powdery mildew starts as a grayish-white patch or mat on the tops of the leaves. It's caused by a fungus that overwinters on plant debris. It produces spores in the spring that are spread by the wind. As it spreads, the leaves can become completely covered and distorted. The time to be on the lookout is in cloudy, humid conditions when days are warm and nights are cool.

RUST
While more prevalent in western gardens, rust is a fungal disease worth including here. You can recognize it by its red/orange dots that start appearing on the undersides of leaves. As it continues to spread, you will see yellow blotches on the tops of leaves. It sometimes appears on canes as well. It develops on leaves that are wet for a prolonged period of time. You should be on the lookout for it in cool, moist weather, especially in rainy, foggy, or misty conditions.

TIP: Select disease-resistant roses in the first place.

Blackspot.

Powdery mildew.

Rust.

Downy mildew.

TIP: Many roses become more immune to disease over time.

DOWNY MILDEW

Common in coastal gardens, you can recognize this by the irregular, purple-reddish spots and blotches on the rose leaves. As the disease advances, it will produce yellowing of leaves, which then turn brown. Frequently, there are dead areas of leaf within the purple blotches. If it is a severe outbreak, you will see purple blotches on the canes. It occurs under cool, moist, cloudy conditions. It can go from mild to severe in as little as three days, so it's important to jump on it quickly if it shows up.

When to Start Treatment

The answer to this is simple. When you have an outbreak of a disease, and you think it's starting to get out of hand, it's time to get help—in the same way as when you sense that your cough is about to turn into pneumonia and realize a visit to the doctor is in order. You should only intervene when you feel you have a potential outbreak on your hands.

So what defines a bad outbreak? When an individual rose has more than about 20 percent of its leaves infected, and you notice it starting to spread to your other roses. The exception is downy mildew. You want to jump on this at the very first sign because it can spread so rapidly.

Should you examine each rose every day? No. I use what I call the "canary in a coal mine" method of detection. Miners used to carry canaries down into the mines because if dangerous gases leaked into the mine, they would kill the canary before the miners. It served as an early warning system. Identify your "canary in a coal mine" rose. It's the rose (or area of the garden) that tends to get disease before any others. Check it when you are

out and about doing normal garden chores. When you notice disease on your "canary in a coal mine" rose, that is your early warning that conditions are right for disease to breed and spread. Then watch your other roses, and if it spreads to them, it's time to step in.

"But I'm only planting disease-resistant roses, so I won't have a 'canary in a coal mine' rose!" you may lament. Well, we all have a rose that isn't overly healthy because it was Mom's favorite, it was a gift from a friend, or we just love the bloom regardless of how the bush looks. If you don't, do what the vineyards in France do, which is to plant disease-prone roses at the ends of the rows of grapes because when those roses get disease, they know it's time to spray the grapes. If nothing else, go buy yourself a diva rose, plant it in a corner of the garden, and let it be your early warning system.

How to Prevent Disease

Basically, everything I've talked about so far in the book will help you prevent rose disease. Following is a summary of the simple steps. Starting with them will give you plants so healthy that you will rarely ever need to intervene.

- Select disease-resistant roses in the first place. I know this may sound obvious, but don't laugh. We all get seduced by those beautiful photos of rose blooms in catalogs, on websites, and in books. Make sure you also pay attention to the comments about how disease resistant they are.
- Create a living soil profile. We talk about this in the planting chapter (see pp. 31, 44–45) and throughout

TIP: If you need to intervene, do so on a onetime basis, the exception being for downy mildew.

A 'Shropshire Lad' climbing rose.

the book. I cannot stress enough the importance of this for preventing disease. A living soil profile greatly enhances your rose's ability to take up nutrients in the soil and use them to enhance its own immune system.

- Mulch using the two-layer method presented in the mulching section (see pp. 50–51). This helps prevent disease by helping to maintain your living soil profile.
- Use slow-release, natural, and organic fertilizers. All of these types of fertilizers feed roses slowly over time by releasing nutrients on a steady basis.

- Be smart in your watering. Overwatering can weaken roses, so be sure to read the section on watering (see pp. 54–57).

If you don't get regular rains, occasionally wash your roses with a garden hose or overhead watering. Many disease spores take up to 24 hours to attach to a leaf once they land on it. Overhead watering can wash them off before they do so. Just do it early enough so everything dries off well before nightfall.

What to Do If Disease Occurs

First, don't panic. With black spot, rust, and powdery mildew, you have a little time to see if the outbreak is mild enough for the roses to handle it on their own—a week or so. During that time, you can do some simple things before you decide it's time to intervene. First, pick off the diseased leaves on the worst plants and get them out of the garden. Do not compost them, since spores can spread to other plants. Instead, put the infected leaves into a plastic bag and throw them away. Sometimes this simple step will prevent disease from spreading. Second, observe the rest of the roses. If they don't get infected, you have it under control.

However, if the disease continues to spread, it's time to intervene on a onetime basis. Notice I said "onetime basis." This doesn't mean you keep doing it. You jump in, give your roses a onetime helping hand, and then let them continue to deal with it on their own. It's just like a course of antibiotics for a bad infection.

Another thing to mention here is that garden roses actually build up disease resistance as they mature. Think of children. When they are young and have never been exposed to things like colds and flu, they have little resistance to illnesses. As children mature, attend kindergarten, and start playing with other kids in the neighborhood, they become exposed to illnesses and catch them all. Yet, this act of catching the disease allows the body to begin to learn what to guard against and how to deal with it. Over time, the child catches fewer and fewer colds. It's the same with many roses. When they are young, they catch every cold in the garden. As they get older, they build up their immunity.

As previously mentioned, however, the exception to all of this is downy mildew. In this instance, panic! This spreads so fast and can kill roses so quickly you need to intervene immediately over the entire garden. I'll tell you more on how to do this in a bit.

HOW TO TREAT IT

Whether it's rust, black spot, powdery mildew, or downy mildew, the treatment is the same. To intervene, we are going to use a product we'll discuss in the chapter on pruning: liquid sulfur. It's sometimes sold as dormant

TIP: The infected leaves won't repair themselves after a spraying of sulfur. Either pick them off or let them yellow and fall off.

lime and sulfur spray. Sulfur is a "contact eradicant." This means it kills almost all diseases shortly after it comes into contact with them. To apply the sulfur, you use a pump or hose end sprayer. Dilute the product to 1 tablespoon per gallon of water. *Do not* add anything else! Particularly, do not use a spreader/sticker, which is a product such as horticultural oil that is designed to keep the product on the leaves. We want the opposite. We want to be able to wash the sulfur off, because on a sunny day it can burn the leaves. It's best to apply it early in the morning or on a cloudy day. After application, you should wait about 15 to 30 minutes, and then wash it off. By that time, the sulfur has done its job. Applying it right before a rainfall also works great, because then it's washed off by the rain.

Generally, a onetime application is all that is needed. Watch the roses, and if the disease continues to spread—and only if it continues to spread—you may need to intervene one more time a week to 10 days later. While this will kill the living disease spores, some of the symptoms will still be there. In the case of black spot, the spots will remain and the leaves may yellow and fall off. It's the same for rust. Powdery mildew actually goes from white to gray when it dies, so you will see visual evidence it's dead. But it's likely the leaves will also eventually fall off. So don't expect the leaves that had disease to clear up. They won't. But the disease will be dead and it won't spread.

One more word on downy mildew: As mentioned previously, jump on it quickly and thoroughly. In this case, spray the entire garden with sulfur and try to get infected parts of the roses out of the garden ASAP. In

An adult hoverfly.

Aphids.

Thrips (the smaller brown insects) on a rose bloom with a variety of the assassin bug.

TIP: The key is balance— a balance between good insects and bad ones.

extreme cases, this might even mean pruning all the roses back hard and removing all debris. And always follow up the first sulfur spray with another one a week later.

As mentioned earlier, I am covering the most basic diseases here. If you have something on your roses you aren't sure about, go to the many good rose forums available (see Resources on p. 178). Post photos and you will get help on your specific problem.

Insects

It's common to assume all insects are bad. While some will indeed cause damage to your roses, the fact is many of these are a vital food source for ones that do no harm to roses and are your most valuable allies in controlling the "bad" ones. The key to all of this is balance, which is best illustrated by a link between two of the most common rose "pests": thrips and aphids.

While aphids and thrips occur all season, peak aphid time is generally in early spring, as the roses are setting buds for the first bloom flush. They love the soft, tender spring growth, particularly on the stems of the newly forming buds. They suck the sap out of the stem, causing it to collapse and the bud to fall off. Peak thrip season is later, over the summer, and they are very tiny insects that live inside enclosed plant areas like unopened rose blooms. In the blooms, they feed on the petals, leaving small holes and even discoloration. For purposes of our illustration, the link between those two insects is a little bug called the hoverfly, which is a very beneficial insect to have in your garden because it doesn't harm roses and loves to eat aphids, thrips, and other insects that may harm roses.

A Delicate Balance

In early spring, Mama hoverfly times the laying of her eggs to the start of aphid season. This is to make sure her offspring have plenty of food on hand as they hatch and mature. As they mature, they go through three stages, feeding voraciously through all of them. In the first stage, they eat smaller insects like the peak spring crop of aphids, plus other smaller insects that may be present, like mites and thrips. At the next two stages, they eat larger prey and then change into adults, at which time they feed on nectar and pollen from flowers.

As time goes on, a later generation subsequently lays their larvae, and once again Mama has her timing down just right. This generation is once again timed to hatch when there will be an abundant food source in the form of—you guessed it—the summer peak crop of thrips plus aphids, mites, and more.

If you get aphid infestations, it could be precisely because you spray for them. You're not attracting beneficial insects, because they have nothing to eat. Would you go to a restaurant with no food? If you have a thrip infestation, it might also be because you sprayed for the aphids, and the hoverflies never laid the next generation of eggs that would have controlled the thrips at their peak time. And if you sprayed for thrips, yet another generation of hoverflies will have nothing to eat and won't lay the eggs that hatch and help you the next time aphid season peaks—not to mention all the other insects they feed on all year. Instead of solving the problem by spraying insecticides, you are actually creating it!

The same applies for many other interdependent relationships in the insect world. If we take away aphids, the ladybugs that also love spring aphids don't show up and lay the eggs that later will hatch the ladybug larvae that feed on thrips and spider mites (small mites that weave webs on the underside of rose leaves and feed on

Hoverfly larvae eating an aphid.

Ladybug larvae, like their parents, are also beneficial in the garden.

Lacewing.

Marmalade hoverfly.

TIP: Create a "host environment" for all the insects, birds, and mammals that will help control the bad ones.

the leaves) that peak when the weather gets hot and dry. Lacewings also love spring aphids and feed on spider mites, thrips, and other bad insects. The fact is there is a veritable beneficial insect army ready to jump in and help as you long as you give them nice barracks to live in and a good chow line.

The best thing to do is stop spraying insecticides and give your garden a few seasons to come back into balance. Insecticides don't discriminate between "good" and "bad" insects. They just kill them all. So yes, the first season you may have more aphids than you care for. But over time, you will achieve a nice balance. I know this works, because I never need to use insecticides—not even organic ones. As with disease, there is no one silver bullet, but if you create the right environment, the roses and nature will do the rest.

The most important thing to take away from this is that even though we use terms like "good" bugs and "bad" bugs, in reality there are no "bad" bugs. Each in its own way is a vital part of keeping our garden healthy, and that makes them all good bugs!

How and When to Handle an Outbreak

There are two basic types of insects you will encounter on roses: soft-bodied insects like aphids, spider mites, and thrips, and hard-bodied insects like Japanese beetles.

The thing to do if you have an outbreak of soft-bodied insects is nothing. Ironically, it's the best thing that can happen, because it will quickly bring beneficial insects

into your garden and actually restore the balance quicker. In the long term, and for purposes of our overall goal of restoring the balance, no action is best.

That being said, I know in the short term it's difficult to sit back and watch your spring bloom being devastated by aphids even though you know in the long run it's for the best. Our minds tell us we shouldn't do anything, but our gardener's heart can't stand it. So if your finger is itching to pull out the spray bottle and do something, you can do so on a onetime basis using insecticidal soaps as per the directions on the bottle. Still, in doing so, understand that you are actually slowing the process of restoring the balance.

SOFT-BODIED INSECTS

Insecticidal soaps are available from your local garden center under a variety of brands. You can even make your own using Dawn® dishwashing liquid at 2 to 3 tablespoons per gallon of water. A small pump sprayer or even a handheld bottle with a spray nozzle is all you need to apply insecticidal soaps. Rather than spraying the entire garden, focus on the area or plants with the worst outbreak. Your goal is not to kill all the bad insects, but to kill enough to bring them in balance with the beneficial ones. Unlike chemicals that kill all insects, insecticidal soaps smother the soft-bodied insects like aphids but leave the hard-bodied ones (like most beneficial insects) alone. But remember, if you can handle it, your garden will come into balance quicker if you let nature run its course and don't intervene.

I realize you're probably doubting that, and I can understand why, but take the advice of my friends at Bierkreek Nursery in the Netherlands, which is one of the

This isolated planter quickly became a balanced environment.

few EU-certified organic rose nurseries in Europe. When they first started with organics, they felt it would be good to intervene occasionally for a bad outbreak using insecticidal soaps. Over time, they realized it was doing more harm than good, and they completely stopped using them. Within a season, balance was restored, and now they use nothing—and this in a working rose nursery with display gardens and fields of hundreds of thousands of roses.

In the photo from Bierkreek Nursery on the facing page, it seems there would be no beneficial insects within miles. Yet, in the very first season of planting roses in this concrete container outside of his home, Hans Van Hage (one of the co-owners of the nursery) observed and photographed more beneficial insects than he'd ever seen. Think about it—if bugs like aphids, thrips, and spider mites can find their way to a concrete pot in the middle of a city, then the beneficial insects like Mama hoverfly can, too. After all, we've already proven Mama H. is one smart bug!

So, I took their advice, stopped spraying anything, and went cold turkey on even the insecticidal soaps. I've never regretted it!

JAPANESE BEETLES

We should take a moment to talk about Japanese beetles. These are shiny bugs that emerge in midsummer from larvae that were hatched in the ground. They are voracious feeders on many plants, but particularly roses. They eat the leaves, the buds, and the flowers. While they occur mostly in the eastern part of the United States, there are some reports of them out West. Also, outside of a few birds, there are not a lot of natural predators in our

TIP: Early flowering plants with good nectar are important for the adult good bugs at the start of the season.

Japanese beetles.

Natural Ways to Deal with Pests

The best way to deal with pests is to help nature achieve that balance. To this end, there are a few things you can do:

- Learn to identify beneficial insects in your area. There is no point in mistakenly killing the good guys.
- Create a "host environment" for beneficial insects. This refers to the plants and areas where they like to live. This will attract more beneficials to your garden and give them a place to rest between snacking on the bad guys. Host plants can be planted right in with your roses.
- If you live in an area with bats, put up bat houses. A female bat will eat her own weight in insects every day!
- Many birds feed voraciously on insects, so put up some birdhouses and make sure the birds have food and water.

TIP: If, while balance is being restored, you feel you have to do something, insecticidal soaps are OK in moderation. Just be aware you may be delaying the natural process.

country since they are not native here. Because Japanese beetles are not native and have no natural predator in the United States, waiting for nature to take care of them is not really an option. Also, since they are hard-bodied insects, insecticidal soaps don't work on them. In the western part of the United States, there is another insect called the Hoplia beetle, which for all practical purposes is similar to the Japanese beetle and should be treated as such.

If you want to protect your roses from them, you can use neem oil (an oil derived from the neem tree that you can purchase through mail order or from many garden stores) after they arrive.

There are also some new cedar-based liquid products coming out that work very well. As with cedar chests for clothes, the scent of the cedar repels the Japanese beetles. They are liquid concentrates made from cedar that you dilute with water and spray on the roses after the beetles arrive. I've used a few and they work. They are not yet widely available, but some mail-order companies are stocking them.

A homemade recipe is to place a few pieces of cedar wood in a bucket of water and pour a gallon of boiling hot water over it. Allow it to soak overnight, put it in a sprayer, and spray it on the foliage in your garden (and on the beetles). You will need to apply it once a week or so during the four- to six-week midsummer Japanese beetle season. Instead of cedar wood, you can use cedar bedding

for animals and pour the boiling water over that to get the liquid. But it has to be in liquid form. Merely placing pieces of cedar around the garden won't help!

Another product that works on Japanese beetles is a liquid containing Milky Spore bacteria, which can be bought in your local garden store or farm supply store, or even through mail order. Despite its scary-sounding name, it's harmless to beneficial insects, birds, bees, pets, and humans. It's applied to the ground in early spring. The nematodes from the Milky Spore attack the Japanese beetle grubs while they are still in the ground, before they fly around the garden. This product works, but it takes a few years to fully take effect. Plus, if you live in a suburban area, you will need to talk your neighbors into applying it to get enough coverage.

What *doesn't* work are those Japanese beetle traps. These are bags you hang around your garden that contain a pheromone that lure the beetles into your garden. They attract far more beetles then the traps can handle and in some cases actually increase the number of beetles in your garden.

Squishing Japanese beetles on the ground has the same effect as the traps. The female Japanese beetle, when squished, emits the same pheromone the traps do, and every male beetle in the area thinks it's party time at your garden!

Disease and Insect Myth Busters

Myth: Roses need regular spraying. They don't. Just as you don't need to take antibiotics 365 days a year, neither do your roses. Allow roses to use their own natural disease-fighting abilities.

Myth: Roses are prone to disease. Yes, some are. And thankfully, many of these are being taken off the market. Garden roses—from old to new—are garden roses because they are naturally resistant to disease. Our job is to help them be even more so through nutrition. The best tool to use when faced with a disease-prone rose is a shovel.

Myth: Some roses are "disease proof." There is no such thing as a disease-proof rose—or a disease-proof plant, animal, or human for that matter. All roses will get some disease if the conditions are right. If you only want disease-proof roses, then I suggest plastic ones!

Myth: The more you spray, the less disease your roses will have. We are finding this to be counterintuitive. In actuality, the more you spray, the more you hinder the rose's ability to fight off disease on its own. Roses, like all plants, produce beneficial pathogens (fungus fighters) on their leaves. Think of these as beneficial insects that eat bad insects. Beneficial pathogens help plants handle disease by destroying bad disease pathogens when they show up in the garden. Our job is to help the good guys do that through soil nutrition, plant nutrition, and proper care techniques.

Additionally, just as chemical insecticides can't tell the difference between beneficial and bad insects, chemical fungicides can't tell the difference between beneficial and bad pathogens. They just kill them all. Constantly spraying roses with chemical fungicides continually reduces the number of beneficial pathogens. When their coverage drops below 80 percent, the rose is no longer able to ward off disease on its own.

Myth: You should spray at the first sign of insects. No, you shouldn't. Many of those insects fill an important role in dealing with other insects later in the season.

Green lacewing.

Be Proactive

Again, when it comes to rose care, it's all interrelated. Roses have natural disease-fighting fungi, and the best way to help them do their job is through good nutrition—nutrition that comes from good soil, proper watering, and feeding. Bad insects also have natural enemies, and creating a host environment for them to live and feed in means they will be ready, willing, and able to help you when the bad guys show up.

So don't think of constantly fighting nature with chemicals. Instead of living in fear of what might happen, give your roses and your garden the tools they need to handle disease and insects on their own. Be proactive instead of reactive!

TIP: Don't cut back perennials, grasses, and other ornamental plants in the fall so that the "good guys" can overwinter in them.

Creating a Host Environment

The best way to control pests on your rose plants is the natural way. Ladybugs love to eat aphids and spider mites. Hoverflys eat aphids and thrips. Lacewings eat all of them. Birds are also voracious feeders on insects, as are small mammals such as bats. Attracting them to your garden is the first step, but what's more important is keeping them there by creating a "host environment."

Simply put, it means if you give the good guys food, water, somewhere to raise their young, and a place to overwinter, they will happily go to battle for you when the bad bugs show up. Best of all, it's not complicated or expensive.

ATTRACTING BENEFICIAL BUGS

The first step is to entice them with something to eat and drink. The drink is water, which can be contained in bird baths, a pond, or a water feature. Just make sure the water doesn't contain chemicals like chlorine. In the case of food, it is already present in your garden in the form of aphids, spider mites, thrips, and the other bad bugs you don't want in your garden. But since the bad guys aren't there all season, you'll need to provide other food sources, also known as "host plants." These are plants that the beneficial insects love as food and shelter. From a food standpoint, the most important plants are the ones that provide a very early food source for the beneficial bugs—before the bad show up in spring.

Water is a vital part of the host environment.

A simple box nest for mud dauber wasps (Trypoxylon).

These early food plants are commonly found in the families of early blooming herbs with good nectar. Examples are some plants from the Brassicia and Umbelliferae families such as mustard, dill, and parsley. Another great family of plants are the early-blooming asters. *Aster solidago* is particularly good for hoverflies. The types of early food plants will vary widely by region, but the key is that they should be early flowering with good nectar. These will keep your beneficial insects happy and healthy early in the season until the aphid buffet shows up.

Once the beneficial pest controllers are happily eating the food source you and nature are providing, they'll want to lay their eggs in your garden since they know subsequent generations will have plenty to eat. So they lay their eggs right where the insect food source like aphids and thrips is, or is going to be—that's in your roses! Luckily, your roses are also the perfect host environment for this beneficial bug nursery.

Various plants, as shown in these photos, make up a host environment.

A woodpile makes a great winter home for all kinds of beneficial insects.

As the season winds down, beneficial insects will start looking for a place to overwinter. They need a place to hide that is sheltered, like a woodpile. You can provide this simply by piling old branches and twigs of soft woods like willow, poplar, and ash in a corner of your yard all season long. Come cold season, they will be the perfect winter chalet for a host of beneficial insects. Ditto for rotted trees. The bugs also like to live in rough vegetation, which is simply the host plants that were not cut back in fall. So don't cut back those herbs, perennials, and ornamental grasses just yet. Wait until spring so the good guys can overwinter in them. Ornamental grasses are particularly good living environments for bugs all during the year.

HELPFUL BIRDS

Birds are also excellent allies in your garden. During the season, they eat the bad bugs, but out of season, provide food sources for them like bird feeders. Most of the perennials and herbs that are host plants for beneficial insects set seed in fall, and that is another good food source for birds—not to mention the roses themselves. Rose hips, which are the bright orange berries that appear on your roses in fall, are a favorite food source for birds. To encourage them, simply stop deadheading your roses in early fall. The hips form when the petals of the blooms fall off.

Birds that like to live in shrubs are among the most voracious insect feeders. They prefer shrubs with soft wood and dense foliage, the latter being a great place to hide. The soft wood attracts the insects they like to eat, so it takes the place of a woodpile to overwinter the beneficial insects.

If you live in a more rural area, small mammals like hedgehogs are great allies. And, of course, bats! Provide them with places to live like the woodpile, bat houses, and compost heaps.

In the end, spend a little time researching and asking about who the good bugs and birds are in your area. Provide them with the things they need to eat, live, reproduce, and overwinter. Do so, and you'll have nature's army standing by to tackle any infestation that comes your way.

CHAPTER FIVE

Pruning and Grooming

The thought of pruning and grooming roses is usually enough to send any gardener running for the smelling salts, oxygen, and their favorite copy of *The Overly Complicated Book of Rose Care*. In that substantial tome, they will find strict rules of rose pruning etiquette that must be followed at all costs or else their roses will all die, the rose police will confiscate their secateurs, and they themselves will be banished to the rose gardener's hall of shame!

Before you do that, understand this: The method of severe, strict rose pruning and grooming has one purpose in mind—to produce long-stem cut flowers for the florist industry or rose shows. But does it work for garden roses?

Remember, a garden rose is a full, attractive shrub covered in leaves and blooms. Cutting that beautiful, full bush back every year to three canes that are 18 inches high runs totally contrary to the definition of what a garden rose is in the first place. Would you cut a shade tree back to 5 feet every year? Of course not! Ditto for garden roses. So while that strict type of pruning may be excellent for exhibition and florist roses, it does not work best for garden roses.

Pruning and grooming garden roses is more about understanding how and why they grow the way they do and how pruning encourages their natural attractive growth habit. This is truly a situation where the "why-to" is far more important than the "how-to."

So grab your secateurs, forget about outward-facing bud eyes, and let's get started!

My pruning tools: Loppers, secateurs, a pruning saw, a case, and my well-worn leather gloves.

Things to Know before You Start

First, let's talk about the difference between pruning and grooming. Pruning a rose means cutting back the rose to its healthy canes plus reinvigorating it by removing crossing canes, old canes, dead wood, and weak growth, and it is usually done in late winter or early spring while the rose is dormant. It's a more severe cutting, and our goal is to rejuvenate the rose by encouraging new growth to produce more flowers. Grooming is removing spent blooms and trimming any overgrowth during the growing season. It's a less severe cutting designed to continually shape the rose during the active growing season. While they have

TIP: If you can, spend the extra money for good tools. They are easier to work with and will last a lot longer, making them cheaper in the long run.

some things in common, they are very different actions, though there is some overlap when it comes to tools. Additionally, a basic understanding of how roses grow will also help you better prune and groom your roses.

TOOLS

Essentially, the most important tools you will need for both pruning and grooming are a good pair of gloves and sharp secateurs.

When pruning, loppers and a small garden handsaw—the folding kind—will come in handy. An optional pruning tool is a battery-powered reciprocating saw with a 9- or 12-inch pruning blade. If you have a lot of large canes to get through, it beats the heck out of a small garden handsaw.

HOW ROSES GROW

Before you can prune or groom roses, you need to understand how they grow. By *grow*, I mean the way the rose builds itself up to its mature height. I'm not talking about the "growing habit" a rose is sold under, such as ground cover, shrub, climber, and so on. Instead, I'm talking about the way the plant physically grows in the garden.

Roses grow in three different ways: from the base, by forming a structure, or by climbing. The first two ways mentioned are how bush roses (any rose that is not a climber) grow and can be found in all classes of roses. There is no hard-and-fast rule, like all shrub roses grow new canes from the base and all floribundas grow by building structure. Because of this, pay no attention to a rose's class when you are pruning. Focus on the way the rose grows and prune accordingly.

It's time to take a deep breath. I realize reading about how a rose grows in a book seems confusing, but once you get in front of your roses, it won't be. So read it again while looking at the roses, and the way they grow will quickly become apparent.

Sharpening Tools

You should regularly sharpen your secateurs and loppers. The technique for both is the same and requires a small sharpening stone made specifically for this purpose. (I like the one made by Felco®.)

Step 1. Sharpen the blade. If you are right-handed, hold the secateurs (or loppers) flat in your left hand with the cutting blade resting flat on your palm and the tip pointed to your wrist. Using the stone, sharpen the top of the cutting blade at an angle of approximately 23 degrees by moving the sharpening stone along the blade's edge from the tip to the base of the blade in one smooth motion. Generally, 10 to 15 strokes will do it.

Step 2. Remove the burrs. Turn the secateurs over and again lay them in your hand, but this time with the tip pointed away from your wrist. At a 5-degree angle, move the stone along the blade's edge in the same continuous motion to remove the burrs caused by the sharpening. A few strokes should be all that is needed.

Facing a large rose at pruning time can be intimidating. Relax, it's not as hard as you think!

BUSH ROSES

Let's examine the first of the two ways bush roses grow: by growing new canes from the base. Look at your rose. Can you trace almost all the canes from the base of the plant right up to the top of the plant without them branching off? By branching, I mean forming a Y where two canes fork off in different directions. Does new growth in spring generally start down low and then grow like mad to 4, 5, 6 feet or more? Do these canes flop out of the plant? Do you have to stake them so they don't fall down? If so, then this is the growth habit your rose falls under. If you planted one of these, it likely reached mature height in about one season or so. They grow quickly!

The second of the two ways bush roses grow is by building a structure. Again, look at the bottom of the

> **TIP:** Pruning isn't just for pruning season. Feel free to shape your roses all season long.

plant. Follow a cane upward. Most likely, the cane will fork into two or three canes partway up the plant, often within the first 2 to 3 feet. Follow one of these forks a little farther and there will likely be another fork; follow one of those and there will be another, and so on. You will rarely find one cane that grows straight from the base of the rose to the top without forking. These types of roses grow some, branch out, grow some more, branch out, and so on. These roses grow more slowly and rarely reach mature height in their first season. Instead, they build themselves up over time like scaffolding.

If you are not sure which growth habit your bush rose falls under, then a light hand when pruning at first is best. Observe the bush until the following season. It will indicate what growth habit it is, and as you get more comfortable with roses, it will be easier to see. Remember, your own gardener's instincts are the best judge!

CLIMBING ROSES

All climbing roses grow the same way. First, they put out long canes from the base of the plant that eventually reach the climbing rose's mature height. This can be 8, 10, 15, even 20 feet and more. From these main canes emerge side shoots, sometimes called laterals, and on the tips of these the blooms are borne. Climbing roses need to establish the mature height of their main canes before they flower, which is why many don't bloom much in their first and second year.

Pruning Roses

If you've never, or rarely, pruned roses, it's pep talk time! You are a gardener. You've trimmed hedges, worked with perennials, shaped up azaleas, and cut the grass. And the result was always the same. Everything grew back. In fact, days, weeks, months, or a year later, you had to trim it again because it grew. Here is a little secret. Roses behave just like all those other plants. You trim and they grow. So forget about making a mistake. If something doesn't go quite right, the rose will shrug it off, grow back, and give you another shot at it. If you are unsure, err on the side of caution, but don't do so because you are worried about mistakes.

Pruning Basics

Pruning garden roses is another one of those chores to which you shouldn't put a calendar date. Each year is different in how quickly spring comes or how long winter will last. Pruning too early in colder climates can be risky because a sudden warm spell can spur new growth, and a sudden freeze afterward can kill it. As with most things in gardening, it's best to let nature tell us when it's time to do things. For this reason, if you live in a climate with a true dormant season, I suggest you prune when the forsythia start to bloom, which is usually around March or April. Another guide you can use if you live in a true dormant season is to start your pruning about six to eight weeks before your last frost date. But since frost dates also vary from year to year, forsythia is really a great natural guide.

If you don't have a dormant season, you have some flexibility. In a climate like coastal southern California, with mild winters and not overly hot summers, the generally accepted time is late December into January, just before the weather starts to warm up. Which brings us to pruning in a climate with a very hot summer and no winter, like mid- to southern Florida, southern Texas, and southern Arizona, for instance. In climates like these,

The rose 'Laure Davoust' grown with an informal support.

which have a very hot summer, the roses actually shut down during the intense heat and become semi-dormant. The cooler months of December and January are peak bloom for a lot of these areas. Because of this, many rose gardeners in these climates are starting to prune in summer, so July and August are ideal. There's no point in cutting your roses back in December or January if that's their peak bloom. Keep in mind the times I noted are best for doing your hard pruning. As I'll discuss in grooming, you can lightly shape your roses all season long.

  VIEW INTRODUCTION TO ROSE PRUNING AT WWW.EVERYDAYROSES.COM.

I've mentioned it before in part 1, but there is no correct height for pruning garden roses. Their use in the landscape and mature size determines height. That being said, here are a few rules of thumb to think about when pruning.

Make sure you are cutting down to the good, healthy growth. If you leave a rose with lots of twiggy growth at the top, next year's bloom show won't be as good. So cut low enough to get to the good stuff. For most garden roses, the minimum thickness of a cane should be about as thick as a pencil. Exceptions are some of the smaller roses like the Drift roses, miniature roses, and some ground covers. If very little of the growth on a rose is thicker than a pencil, just use your instincts to look for healthy growth.

Some roses bloom in sprays. Instead of a single bloom on a stem, there are multiple blooms on one stem. Think of a candelabra. On these roses, make sure you cut to below the point where all the flower stems emanate from on the main cane, just below the "base" of the candelabra. Leaving all those little flowering stems will result in an odd-shaped plant. Best to cut the entire spray off.

For garden roses, don't reduce their mature size by more than about a third to half of the mature height of the plant. They really don't like hard pruning down to 18 inches. This is why it's so important to think about the rose's use in the landscape before you even buy it. If you want the rose to be short, buy a short one. If you want it to be tall, make sure you buy a tall one.

Now, that you know the pruning basics, let's get started.

Pruning Bush Roses

Following are steps that are best to start off with for bush roses, regardless of which of the two ways it grows. Climbing roses have their own basic steps, and we'll cover those on pp. 89–91. If at first you aren't sure if you should cut a cane or branch, leave it and come back to it later. It's easier to cut something later than it is to glue it back on!

When I teach pruning classes, I always tell people to start with clearing out dead wood. It's dead, so you can't make a mistake. It's also logical, simple, and something every gardener already knows they should do. The rest just flows from there.

Then, cut out weak and damaged growth. David Stone of Mottisfont Abbey in the United Kingdom, my pruning mentor, calls these the "twiggy bits." Said with a cup of tea and a British accent, it's quite a delightful phrase that fits perfectly. Twiggy bits are weak, straggly growth, small growth, or remnants of flower stems that didn't fall off. When you take this off, as when you remove dead growth, the bush reveals its shape and the way it grows. Notice I did not use the phrase *thin growth*. Some garden roses have healthy growth that's thinner than a pencil, so thin growth isn't always twiggy bits in roses. Focus more on weak and straggly than thin. If you aren't sure, leave it and come back to it.

Identify damaged canes. Are any canes broken or torn? If so, they need to go. For now, cut just below the damage and remember that cane. Tie a piece of ribbon around it if need be. We want to remember it because later we may choose to take it out completely from the base of the plant.

Look for obvious crossing canes. A crossing cane is one that is growing on one side of the plant's base and shoots across the bottoms of other canes to come out the other side of the plant. Generally, they are making contact with other canes, rubbing, and causing damage.

Climbing rose Raspberry Cream Twirl™.

How to Prune a Bush Rose

Start by cutting out dead canes all the way at the base of the plant.

Twiggy bits can often be found in the middle of the plant. This is where your loppers come in handy.

Damaged canes go next.

Remove a crossing cane.

Decide your final pruning height and cut away everything above that.

Always double-check your work.

Lower the outer canes on a rose that grow from the base.

The obvious ones come out. The unobvious ones stay in. You can come back and cut them out later as part of the final touch-up. Sometimes it's easier to make a decision after everything else has been pruned away. Here is a little hint if you are still unsure how your rose grows: If you have several crossing canes, it's likely that you have a rose that grows new canes from the base. If you don't, it's likely you have a rose that builds a structure. But notice I said "likely." Don't make your mind up yet. Additionally, don't confuse crossing canes with those coming straight up in the middle of the plant. The old-school method was to cut out canes in the middle of the plant for "air circulation." On garden roses, we want a nice, full look, so it's OK to leave canes in the middle of the plant. They form the middle of the top canopy on garden roses. Instead, look for canes that are radically shooting back across the inside of the plant and damaging other canes.

Decide what your final pruning height is going to be. Again, this is determined by what you want the rose to be in your landscape coupled with the guideline of never bringing it down more than a third to half its mature height. For roses that build a structure over time, a third is the most I would advise you to cut. Once you've decided on a final height, bring all the canes down to it. Cut flat across the top of all the canes, and we'll do the final shape later.

Now take a step back, and the way the rose grows should be quite apparent.

Now that you've done the basic pruning for bush roses, it's time to fine-tune your prune. We'll break this down by the two ways bush roses grow: with canes that grow from the base and with canes that build a structure.

PRUNING CANES THAT GROW FROM THE BASE

As we mentioned before, these types of roses often have canes that grow up and flop about, often flopping right out of the plant. The instinct is to stake or tie them up for support. But there is a way to use the plant's own way of growing to naturally build an outer "cage" to support those floppy canes. It does away with the need for stakes to support them.

New canes on these roses grow from the middle of the plant's base. They grow straight up and are often not able to support themselves when they are young. However, as they age, they stiffen and are then able to support themselves. That is the first key to remember. The other key to remember is that as the canes mature and stiffen, the base of each individual cane literally moves from the middle of the base of the plant toward the outer edge of the plant's base. That's right, they physically shift from the middle to the outer edge of the plant's base. They do this to make room for new canes that will grow from the middle of the base. The before-mentioned David Stone figured out how to use this to our advantage.

With both types of bush roses, finish by shaping.

David realized that as these canes become self-supporting and move to the outer edge of the base, they can be pruned to encourage growth that will naturally form a cage around the outside of the plant that supports the newer canes and prevents them from falling all over the place. This happens because when you trim a rose cane back, several of the bud eyes just below the cut will sprout branches. Because bud eyes are found on all sides of the cane (in a spiral staircase pattern), they fan out like the fingers of an outstretched hand. This outstretched hand literally "catches" the younger canes if they try to fall out of the plant.

So our first step in finishing pruning these types of roses is to go all around the outer part of the plant and cut the mature, stiff canes on the outside of the plant down another 6 inches or so. The side branches that will emerge will extend out 6 to 10 inches, so cut a mature stiff cane every foot or so. This way, the "outstretched fingers" will touch each other, leaving no way out for those unruly younger canes. If you are doing this for the first time on your rosebush, you will not fully surround the plant with a cage the first year you prune this way, nor maybe even

the second. There will be gaps because you've pruned a different way previously or simply because the rose is too young. But over a few seasons, more outer canes will grow to become part of the cage.

As a final step, if you had any damaged canes in the center and the cut you made below the damage is 1 foot or lower than the rest of the canes, cut them out at the base of the plant. If you leave them, they will just branch out and create a thicket in the middle of the plant. If they are on the outer edge and you can make them part of the cage, by all means go ahead. If you can't, take them out.

At this point, we are done pruning canes that grow from the base. Do a little light, logical shaping to get the top of the plant into a rounded mushroom cap shape and admire your work.

 VIEW PRUNING ROSES THAT GROW CANES FROM THE BASE AT WWW.FINEGARDENING.

PRUNING ROSES THAT BUILD A STRUCTURE

Roses that build a structure require very little additional pruning other than what was mentioned in "Pruning Bush Roses" on pp. 85–88. The canes on these roses are self-supporting, so you don't need to encourage them to create a cage. As I've mentioned, these roses take time to grow, so a lot of hard pruning will set them back. Just spend a little time trimming, rounding, and shaping to please your own eye, and you are essentially done. If you see damaged canes on these types of roses, make a nice, clean cut below the damaged area and leave the cane in. The bud eyes below the fork will sprout and branch out, which is good for this kind of rose because that is the way it naturally grows!

  VIEW PRUNING ROSES THAT BUILD A STRUCTURE AT WWW.FINEGARDENING.COM.

TIP: Always cut out deadwood when you see it, regardless of the plant's age.

Pruning Climbing Roses

Pruning climbing roses is actually quite simple. It's almost easier than pruning bush roses. The key is to understand that climbing roses have two kinds of canes: main canes, which grow from the base of the plant and provide the structure, and lateral canes, which grow out from the main canes and bear the flowers. These laterals grow all along the main cane. Once you understand how to tell each apart and what their job is, how to prune a climbing rose quickly reveals itself.

The essence of pruning climbing roses is never to cut the main canes back. You can trim the laterals to your heart's content—even during the growing season. The reason you don't cut the main canes hard each year is because you won't get much in the way of flowering the following season. Climbing roses grow to their mature size in the first year and bloom in subsequent years, which I discuss more in depth in "Working with Climbing Roses" (pp. 102–103). For this reason, if you cut the main canes back every year, they will put all their energy into growing back at the cost of the blooms.

The lateral canes are another story. You can trim them back to within 12 inches of the main canes and they will continue to flower. In fact, doing so encourages them to flower, which is another reason to do so after each bloom flush.

Pruning above the Bud Eye

You should make your cut ½ inch above the bud eye. This is a good rule of thumb to follow. If you make the cut too high, the cane may die back to the bud eye. Too low, and you run the risk of damaging the bud eye. Once you've made a cut, seal it with all-purpose glue to keep out pests. This keeps burrowing pests like cane borers from drilling down into your canes and setting up homestead. I would advise sealing the ends for canes that are thicker than a pencil. For thinner canes, it's not necessary.

Making your cuts ½ in. above a bud eye is best.

TIP: Take out weak or damaged growth. Just trust your gardener's instincts to recognize branches that aren't full of vigor. This also better helps you to see the plant's structure.

Before you know it, you're done!

The other reason to continually trim the laterals is to keep the rose attractive. We've all seen a tidily pruned rose at the start of the season turn into a waving, knotted mess by midsummer. It has canes long enough to snag everyone that walks by. It's the untrimmed laterals that create that thicket. Trimming them after each bloom flush keeps the rose in check. With that in mind, let's get started.

  VIEW PRUNING AND CONTROLLING A CLIMBING ROSE AT WWW.FINE GARDENING.COM.

HOW TO PRUNE CLIMBING ROSES

First, step back and look at the structure of the plant. Identify the main canes and lateral canes. Do you see any gaps in the plant that should be filled by a main cane, but there isn't one available? In that case, you can fill in that gap by turning a lateral cane into a main cane. If you identify such a gap, read "Converting a Lateral to a Main Cane" on p. 92. If not, then read on.

Once you've identified the main canes, pick one and begin trimming the laterals, starting at the bottom of the plant and working your way up the cane. Trim each lateral (except those you are turning into main canes) back to within 1 to 2 feet in length. How long or short depends again on the rose's use in the landscape. If it's on an arbor over a walkway, you will want to cut to 1 foot so it doesn't quickly get out of control and snag passersby. If it's on a fence and you want a looser look, leave them longer. By all means, you can leave them to 3, 4, 5 feet if you like.

When you are done with that first main cane, step back and once again look at the plant. Recheck the laterals you are keeping as main canes and decide if you want to add some or take some away. Then pick the next main cane and work your way up, trimming laterals as you go. Repeat those steps until you are done. The reason you want to step back and reexamine the plant between main canes is because when you are cutting in the middle of a climber, you cannot see the big picture. Trust me, I know this from personal experience! I've often accidentally cut laterals I meant to keep long when I was in the middle of the plant trimming. But the rose kept growing, and the next year I had a second chance to get it right.

Once you are done, take one last step back, look for parts you may have missed, and then trim for aesthetics.

Main canes grow from the base and provide the structure.

If the rose needs retraining onto whatever structure you are using to support it, this is by far the best time to do so.

For damaged canes on climbing roses, you have two options: If the damage is on the lower half of the cane, take the cane out at the base and the rose will quickly replace it with a new one. If the damage is on the top half of the cane, make a clean cut below the damage. The bud eyes below the damage will sprout new canes, and you can simply treat them the same way you would as when turning a lateral into a main cane.

TIP: Never worry about making a pruning mistake. The canes will grow back.

Converting a Lateral to a Main Cane

There are times when you need to fill in a gap because the climbing rose plant was damaged or grew oddly. To do this, you can turn a vigorous lateral cane into a main cane. By vigorous lateral, I mean one that is long, is thick, and is outgrowing the others. In many instances, these laterals grow so energetically they never have blooms.

Doing this is simple. First, identify the ones you want to convert—you may want to tie some brightly colored ribbon around them so that you don't accidentally cut them. Make sure the lateral you are converting has never been cut before. It should be one long, continuous length of growth. If it has been cut, it won't grow longer, but instead the bud eyes at the tip will sprout and make a mess—so ignore those and seek a new one. Then, gently lay the long lateral cane against whatever structure you will be tying the rose to—a trellis, fence, arbor, and so on. Tie it in using a soft plant tie or your preferred method, and begin treating it like a main cane, keeping it trained in that area between horizontal and 45 degrees (for more detail, see "Working with Climbing Roses" on pp. 102–103). Over time this lateral (now a main cane) will continue to grow, and the bud eyes along it will sprout new laterals. When that happens, throw it a little graduation party. It's now a main cane!

Laterals grow off the main canes and bear the flowers.

Rejuvenating an Old Rose Plant

There comes a time in a rose cane's life when it gets old and stops producing healthy growth for new flowers. In other words, it's "bloomed out." You can recognize these canes because they are heavily wooded over with bark, the only new growth they put out is weak and spindly, and almost all the bud eyes along them have sprouted and flowered at one point. You generally start seeing them after the rose's fifth year. If you leave it, the cane will simply take up energy that could be better used elsewhere in the plant. There is no rule on how often you should do this. Instead, let the plant show you when it's time.

If you have an old rose and want to rejuvenate it, you can do so by slowly taking out old canes to spur new ones to sprout and take their place. Simply follow the bloomed-out cane down to ground level and cut it out at the base of the plant using either a pruning saw or battery-powered reciprocating saw. But don't take out a lot of the old canes at once. The first year, take out only one bloomed-out cane, the next year perhaps two (if the plant has thrown out enough new canes from the previous year to take their places). Continue taking out old canes as new ones emerge to take their places.

Are you are getting sweaty palms at even the thought of doing this? Sounds more like butchering than rejuvenating, right? I know. I've been there. The first time I did this I was scared to death I was going to kill the rose. But I did it, and lo and behold, not one, not two, but three new canes came bursting forth. I've never looked back.

VIEW REMOVING AN OLD CANE FROM A ROSE AT WWW.EVERYDAYROSES.COM.

VIEW REJUVENATING AN OLD CLIMBING ROSE AT WWW.EVERYDAYROSES.COM.

A Few More Things about Pruning

Before we leave pruning and go on to grooming, I want to change the way you think about pruning roses. Pruning tends to be a backward-looking chore, when we think of removing last year's growth. Instead, treat it as a forward-looking chore.

For all roses, pruning stimulates new growth. On a rose that grows new canes from the base, the younger canes stiffen, move toward the edge, and can be used to help support the new, younger canes. On climbing roses, this year's laterals can be next year's main canes. And periodically taking out an old cane spurs fresh young growth. Think ahead about what your rose is going to do and need, and pruning becomes something you do for the future of your rose. That's why I don't like to call it "pruning" your roses. I like to call it "rejuvenating" your roses.

PRUNING A NEWLY PLANTED ROSE

Prune newly planted roses as little as possible. They need all the energy they can get, and they get it through the leaves. Pruning them cuts off much of their food source in that first year. So for newly planted roses, do the logical things like cut out deadwood and remove weak, twiggy growth. Don't worry too much about the canes the rose had when you first bought it. By the third or fourth year they will be gone, having been replaced by strong new ones. You should take those first ones out when a new cane can fill in the space.

OCCASIONALLY CUTTING A ROSE BACK HARD

You might see a recommendation to cut a rose, for example a Knock Out, back hard every now and then to renew it and/or keep it under control if it gets really large. Often this is done with hedge shears by simply cutting the entire plant back to 12 inches or so. I have no problems with doing this every now and then. An instance might be when removing old canes creates an unattractive plant. The plant may, over time, grow lopsided or have gaps in it that don't seem to fill in. Sometimes roses grow so quickly that cutting them back by only a third to a half isn't enough to keep them in check. Now *that's* a garden rose!

So if you see or read somewhere that this is recommended for your particular rose, it's fine to do it every

Pruning Rose Roots

While roots are a plant's foundation and the bigger the better, there are times when the roots need some pruning and trimming. How little, or much, you prune them depends on the reason.

BAREROOT ROSES

Damaged Roots: Sometimes roots are damaged or broken in packaging. When you come across these while planting a bareroot rose, simply snip them off just above the damage or break. Don't worry about trimming the other roots to the same length as the damaged one. Leave them alone.

Long Roots: Sometimes the roots are too long for the hole you dug. Try to dig a deeper hole! Kidding aside, I've seen some bareroot roses with ridiculously long roots. It's best not to trim them, but if needed, up to a third is acceptable.

NEW CONTAINER ROSES

Damaged Roots: If you are planting a container rose into the ground and see any damaged roots on the outside of the root ball, snip them off and gently pull them out. Go slowly so you don't accidentally break up the rootball.

Root Bound Rose: Roses that have been in a container too long form a mass of roots tightly knit together. So tight it's sometimes difficult for the roots to grow out into the soil after planting. If you see this, trim away some of the outer roots winding their way around the root ball. Doing so will encourage new root growth, which will grow into the soil.

Pillar roses break up a gravel area at Mottisfont Abbey in the United Kingdom.

now and then when normal pruning doesn't seem to be producing the plant you want. Consider it to be like hitting the "reboot button" on your computer and starting all over again when it locks up and makes you mad.

REMOVING OLD ROSE LEAVES

Some rose enthusiasts feel that leaves harbor fungal spores over winter. They believe that if you leave them on after pruning, come spring those old leaves will infect the new growth, thereby increasing the chances of disease. This is sound theory and a good idea, but not always practical in the case of garden roses. Removing the leaves on a bunch of hybrid tea roses that were cut down to 18 inches tall is no big deal because there aren't many leaves left. Garden roses tend to be pruned taller and, particularly in the case of climbing roses, removing leaves becomes a tedious and long chore. So is there an easier way not only to remove leaves but also rid the roses of overwintering fungal spores?

Thankfully, the answer is yes. The product to use is liquid sulfur, and it comes in a form you dilute with water (see "What to Do If Disease Occurs" on pp. 69–70).

TIP: With garden roses, don't worry about outward-facing bud eyes and five-leaflet leaf sets. Just prune to strong, healthy growth at your desired height. And if you don't know what a five-leaflet leaf set or a bud eye is, don't worry about it. You don't need to know.

Sulfur is a contact eradicant, which is a fancy way of saying it kills fungal spores the minute it hits them. So spraying it will wipe out overwintering fungal spores on old leaves, canes, and the top of the mulch. You can't leave it on during the growing season because it will burn the leaves, but you can use that to your advantage now. At the end of the growing season, if left on the leaves when the sun is out, it will burn the leaves, causing them to fall off but doing no damage to the rose plant. If you add common horticultural oil to it so it sticks to the leaves, it will really burn the leaves, causing most of them to fall off on their own. If any leaves are left, don't bother with pulling them off, because the sulfur will have killed any fungal spores trying to overwinter. Come spring, as the new growth emerges, these "burned" old leaves will fall off on their own to make room for the new.

To apply, pick a sunny day. Purchase both the sulfur and the horticultural oil, mix them as per the directions on the label for dormant spray strength, and douse your recently pruned roses with it, leaves and all. I like those inexpensive hose-end sprayers for lots of roses or a small sprayer if you have just a few. Whatever you use, don't spend a lot of money because you will never get it fully

cleaned out—the oil will cause it to stick to the tank of the sprayer. I dedicate one sprayer and use it from year to year.

As with any product, follow the instructions to the letter and be careful with it. While it is a natural product, it can be messy, and I'd advise wearing gloves and old clothes. And—oh yes—it smells a bit like rotten eggs, so warn your neighbors. After you've finished, wait a week and do it again. It's easy, and no leaf picking is needed.

Pruning Myth Busters

Serious rose folks love to talk about pruning. Many a rose conference has gone well into the night as intense discussions play out over the pruning methods needed to achieve that Queen of Show rose. Over time, many discussions have found their way into general rose care books, and the information in them can be both intimidating and frightening to the average gardener.

As I previously mentioned, if you wish to enter rose shows, those methods are good. But since the vast majority of the people who grow roses just want a nice plant with flowers, those methods are not needed.

Myth: **You must prune to an outward-facing bud eye.** I hear this more than anything else. My favorite response is, "What difference does it make? The rose is outside, therefore they are all outward facing!" (This leads to much scratching of the head.)

By always pruning to an outward-facing eye, each bloom grows outward from the existing ones and minimizes potential damage from rubbing up against each other. The rule exists because of the florist and show rose industry's desire for undamaged roses. If you sell long-stem roses or exhibit roses, this makes sense. But in a garden, we want a mass of blooms all nicely covered. So the outward-facing bud eye rule doesn't apply here.

Myth: **Prune to 18 inches high.** As a general rule, the shorter you prune a hybrid tea rose, the longer the stems will be when it blooms in spring. Since long stems are what you want in a show or florist rose, it makes perfect sense for that purpose.

Garden roses are landscape shrubs. And as with any landscape shrub, the height you prune it to is determined by its use in the garden. If it's a hedge, you leave it tall.

Periodically taking out an old cane results in fresh new ones.

If it borders a walk, you trim it tighter and shorter. The same rule applies to garden roses. There is no "correct" height outside of observing the "don't cut by more than one-third to one-half of the mature height" rule.

Myth: Leave only three to five strong, healthy canes. Long-stem roses require a strong, vigorous base to support them as they grow. Having fewer canes means the rose can focus all its energy on fewer stems and produce that Queen of Show. Fewer flowers also means each individual bloom will be larger. This is why this is a good rule for producing florist and exhibition roses.

Garden roses should have lots of flowers, and we aren't very concerned about bloom size or stem length. So the more healthy canes, the better!

Myth: You can only prune or groom during pruning time. If a garden rose is just another flowering shrub, shouldn't you be able to groom it all year? The answer is yes, you can groom all season long to keep the rose in shape. There is one exception: Don't do the kind of hard cutting that encourages tender new growth close to fall. We don't want that new growth exposed to the first frosts of winter.

Myth: Always cut to a 45-degree angle sloping down away from the bud eye. The 45-degree angle rule came about because it was thought the sap from the cut would run down, covering the desired outward-facing bud eye and causing it not to swell and grow a new long stem. Having the angle slope away from the eye meant the sap would run down the back of the cane and away from the outward-facing eye.

In all my days, I have never seen a bud eye not swell and grow because of being covered by sap. So forget about this rule completely.

Myth: Dip your clippers into a diluted bleach solution to sanitize them between cuts. Seriously? Besides being time-consuming and simply overkill, it's just one more myth that makes some aspects of rose growing sound ridiculous. Does your tree surgeon dip his chain saw in bleach between each cut? Hey, I've got another one: Dip your spoon in hot water between bites of cereal!

Knock Out roses grow along a garden path.

Grooming

Don't confuse grooming and pruning. Pruning, as we just discussed, is preparing your rose for the growing season and is a more severe, once-a-year task. When I talk about grooming your roses, I am talking about maintaining them throughout the growing season by removing old flowers through deadheading, trimming them to influence shape and growth, keeping them tidy, and controlling their size.

Generally, with show roses, both pruning and grooming are reserved for late winter and early spring. With garden roses, this isn't so. While pruning is reserved for late winter and early spring (with the exception of very hot climates as mentioned on pp. 83–84), grooming can be done all season. Garden roses are vigorous by nature, and some of the larger ones can quickly get out of hand if left unchecked for a full season. So treat your garden roses just like any other plant and feel free to groom as needed to keep them tidy.

When to Groom

Any time after a garden rose is finishing a bloom flush is a great time to groom. What is a bloom flush? Even roses that flower all year are never actually in full bloom every day of the season. They peak with flowers, those blooms begin to lose their petals, new buds mature, and the rose peak blooms again. Each peak bloom is called a bloom flush. The first bloom flush is the spring bloom flush. For those of you without a dormant season and a true spring, this would be the first flush after pruning. This first flush is usually followed by rapid growth because the temperatures are still cool enough to encourage it. Right after the spring bloom flush is a great time to get in there, deadhead (cut off old blooms), and groom (trim the rose to shape, cut out deadwood). Then use the period after each subsequent bloom flush as an opportunity to do another deadhead and groom. Waiting until after the flush does not mean waiting until there are no flowers on the rose. Ideally, there will always be some flowers on it. But there are always cycles of lots of flowers, fewer flowers, lots of flowers, fewer, and so on. Some roses have a short time between flushes and some a little longer, so there is no set number of days for all roses.

TIP: Stop grooming six to eight weeks before your first frost date.

You should stop grooming about six to eight weeks before your first frost date in the fall, so you don't encourage tender new growth that can be damaged by a freeze. This could kill or weaken the plant.

Stop deadheading as you get close to fall as well. Many roses set brightly colored hips. These are the orange to reddish "berries" you see on many roses in winter. They can be the size of a pea up to a marble. They form when you don't cut off old flowers and in fact contain rose seeds. As with any plant, a rose wants to reproduce itself. That is part of its survival instinct. A rose flower is the first step in that process. If the rose flower is pollinated by a bee, a bird, or even a human, it stays on the bush, it matures in the fall, and the hip forms around the seeds. A hip is literally a rose seed pod. This is why deadheading encourages reflowering. Cutting off the old flowers signals to the rose it has not fulfilled its reproductive instinct, so it quickly flowers again—more quickly than it would if you left the old blooms on.

Those hips maturing in fall signals to the rose it's done its job and now can go to "sleep" (enter dormancy) for the winter. Without maturing hips on it in fall, it may continue to push new blooms, and that tender growth could be damaged by a frost. We want our roses to go to sleep; hence, we stop deadheading. The hips are decorative, but more important, they are a winter food source for birds—the same birds who next spring will help keep your bad insects under control.

You can do light grooming of a young rose, but keep it to a minimum. Deadheading is OK, but don't do much beyond that—outside of removing deadwood, of course.

 VIEW SUMMER CLEAN-UP AT WWW.EVERYDAYROSES.COM.

Roses, perennials, and shrubs mix in a classic English flower border.

How to Groom Your Roses

Groom your roses as you would any other plant. When you make your cuts, do so above good, healthy growth—about ½ inch above your selected bud eye (the slightly swollen spot where the leaves cluster). Don't worry about cutting at a certain angle or paying attention to which way the bud eye is facing. If you see deadwood, always cut it out.

Don't groom a tall rosebush short. When you groom, cut down no more than a third of the plant's mature height at most. Garden roses don't like being cut hard on a regular basis. Once a year during pruning time is OK, but if you keep doing it all the time, roses seem to sulk by not flowering and not growing. I'm not sure why this is, but it's something I've observed over the years. If you need to keep cutting a tall rose way down all year to keep it in check, you simply planted the wrong rose in that spot. If you wanted a short rose in that spot, you should have planted a short one in the first place! If you find you need to constantly cut the rose down, move the tall plant to a location where it works with your landscape needs.

Grooming is a great time to shape and work with your roses.

INFLUENCING THE DIRECTION OF NEW GROWTH

As your rose matures, you may notice it growing more toward one side. Or a cane may break toward the top, leaving a gap that needs to be filled. There is a way to influence the direction a rose grows in. The key is to understand how the bud eyes work.

Bud eyes are never all on one side of a cane facing in just one direction. Instead, they are found on all sides of the cane and in fact circle up the cane like a spiral staircase. You can use this to your advantage because the new growth that emerges from a bud eye will always grow in the same direction the bud eye is facing.

So if you want to fill a gap in the rosebush, make your cuts ½ inch above bud eyes that face into the gap. The new growth will head into that gap in your rose bush and quickly fill it up.

Timing Rose Blooms for a Special Event

Say you have a backyard wedding or a garden party coming up and you'd love to be able to show off your roses in full bloom. So you ask yourself, is there a way to time the roses so they will bloom on the big day? There is, and it has to do with timing the bloom cycle.

First, let's start by explaining what a bloom cycle is. A bloom cycle is the time it takes the rosebush to produce a flower after you deadhead off an old flower. It starts when you cut off the old flower and ends when the new flower opens up. Cycles vary by rose plant. Timing the entire bloom cycle involves cutting off all flowers and buds so the cycle for the entire bush begins and ends at the same time. Exhibitors do this to get ready for a big show.

I'll tell you how to do it, and then you can use the chart on p. 101 to determine what the bloom cycle is for your particular plant.

HOW TO BEGIN

You do this via normal deadheading techniques. Count down to the second or third leaflet group and make your cut just above it. Make sure you are cutting above healthy, vigorous growth. Now, during normal deadheading, we only have to worry about cutting off the flowers that are faded or no longer have petals. This encourages the bush to constantly replenish itself and gives you a pretty constant bloom over the growing year.

But we are trying to time the bush to cover itself in flowers all at once—not only one bush, but your whole garden. Beautiful? Yes. But it calls for radical surgery to pull it off. All the flowers, new and old, and all the buds have to be cut off. No exceptions. A true expert can play with this rule, but this kind of touch is beyond most of us.

So cut off everything: new buds, new flowers, and old flowers. Then wait for it all to grow back and bloom on the big day. Just remember, the farther down the cane you go, the longer it takes for the blooms to come back. The

TIP: Deadheading will cause your roses to rebloom faster. But they will still rebloom if you don't deadhead.

Roses frame a relaxed seating area in a Palm Desert garden.

general rule of thumb is to add about three to five more days for each additional leaflet group you go down.

To time your blooms, use the chart on p. 101. Look up the type of plant you have and the number of days in the bloom cycle. Find the date of your event on the calendar, count back the numbers of days in the bloom cycle, and make all your cuts then. This chart was written for an average Zone 7. If you are in a cooler climate, add a few days, and in a really warm climate, subtract a few. If you aren't sure, then cut a third of your bushes one day, a third a few days later, and the rest a few days after that. At least something will have flowers!

Just remember the simple rules. Take it all off and make your cuts above the second or third leaflet group. Those are the basics. Now get out there and impress your guests!

Grooming Myth Busters

Hips add winter interest to roses.

Myth: **Always deadhead to a five-leaflet leaf set.** A five-leaflet leaf is defined as a set of leaves containing five full leaves. If you examine the leaves on roses, you will notice each "group" of leaves is attached to the cane by a base—generally at a bud eye. Each group is known as a "set of leaves." Some have three leaves, some five, and some even seven or more. The thinking behind this was that a five-leaflet leaf set was where the cane was thick enough to support that next long-stem bloom. And in the case of many hybrid teas, this does indeed apply. For garden roses it does not. They don't have long stems, so just deadhead to good, healthy growth.

Myth: **Deadhead to an outward-facing bud eye.** As with pruning to an outward-facing bud eye, this meant the next long stem would grow away from the others so as not to damage the show blooms by rubbing up against each other. Again, if you exhibit, this is a good rule. But we want garden roses to be covered in blooms, and if they rub each other, so what? Again, just deadhead to good, healthy growth and forget about which way the bud eye faces.

TIP: As you groom, cut down to healthy growth. Don't worry which way the bud eye faces or how many leaves are on the leaf set.

A five-leaflet leaf set.

Myth: Only trim your roses during pruning season. For garden roses, forget it. As mentioned earlier, feel free to trim during the season to keep the plant in check.

Myth: To get your roses to bloom again, you must deadhead. Let's get real. Roses that have never seen a pair of secateurs bloom well into fall, at which time they stop as the old blooms mature into hips. Deadheading will get them to rebloom quicker, but they will bloom again regardless.

TIP: Bud eyes always grow new canes in the direction the bud eye is facing. Use this to fill in gaps in the plant.

Timing a Rose Bloom

This chart is timed using cuts at the level of the second or third leaflet group below the bloom or bud.

TYPE OF ROSE	NUMBER OF DAYS IN BLOOM CYCLE
BOURBONS	55–60
SHRUBS	Varies, but approx. 50–60
FLORIBUNDAS	50–55
HYBRID MUSKS	55–60
HYBRID PERPETUALS	60–65
HYBRID RUGOSAS	55–60
HYBRID TEA	45–55
MINIATURES	35–40
PORTLANDS	60–65
TEAS	45–50

Working with Climbing Roses

A climbing rose in full bloom is a stunning sight in any garden setting. Like feathers on a Cherokee ceremonial headdress, the blooms drape the plant from top to bottom, adding a stunning visual sight to your landscape. Any gardener who has seen this either in person or in a book dreams of having that vista in their own garden.

Often the reality of what's in the garden falls short of what was first imagined when the rose was planted. Instead of a waterfall of flowers, you end up with blooms mostly on the top of the climber or with a great deal of green growth at the expense of a garland of blooms. For this reason, many gardeners give up on climbing roses and deem the effect not worth the effort.

The key to achieving that arbor clothed in rose blooms is to understand how climbing roses work. Keeping a few simple things in mind when you spend time training your climbing rose in its youth will go a long way toward the photo in the magazine becoming reality in your garden.

HOW CLIMBING ROSES GROW

The first thing to understand is this: Unlike most shrub roses that will grow and bloom in the first year, climbing roses grow first and bloom when they reach mature size. The general pattern is to have a few blooms in the rose's first season, but most of its energy should be spent getting established and developing some top growth. The second season will produce a minor spring flush followed by rampant green growth. The third season is when the rose starts to come into its own and begins to bloom steadily.

The second thing to understand is that climbing roses have two kinds of canes. The first are the main canes. These are the long canes that grow from the base of the plant to the full height of the climbing rose. Like trunks on trees, they form the structure

Weaving canes back and forth at 45-degree angles gives you a wall of flowers instead of just blooms at the top.

that holds up the parts of the climbing rose that bear the leaves and flowers. They can be 8, 12, 15 feet long or more. These are the first canes that grow on a young climbing plant. The other canes are the lateral canes—sometimes also called side shoots. The laterals grow out of the bud eyes on the main canes, bear the flowers generally at their tips, and are thinner than the main canes. They really start to appear after the plant becomes a few years old. Think of them as the small branches on trees that bear the leaves.

The third thing to understand is that if you train all the main canes to climb straight up a structure, they will not produce the laterals that bear the blooms. Instead, they will bloom only at the top of the main canes. It's only when you train the main canes horizontally that those bud eyes sprout laterals all up and down the main canes. And it is at the ends of these dozens and dozens of laterals that the blooms appear. For a climbing rose, "horizontally" means

'Mme. Alfred Carriere' at Mottisfont Abbey in the United Kingdom.

Main canes trained within a horizontal to 45-degree range give you lots of flowers.

anything from purely horizontal to 45 degrees. When trained anywhere in that range, the bud eyes on the main canes will sprout laterals, and you will get a wall of blooms as opposed to a wall of green with a fringe of flowers on top.

TRAINING A ROSE ON A TRELLIS

Assuming you have a standard 4-foot by 8-foot trellis panel made from wood (or other material), plant the rose in the center of the bottom edge of the trellis. As the first main canes grow, train the ones on the left side of the plant toward the left edge of the trellis at a 45-degree angle and the ones on the right side of the plant toward the right edge at a 45-degree angle. As you get additional main canes on each side of the plant, take those straight up for a bit and then angle them off to the sides. Try to keep the angled canes about 18 to 24 inches above each other. This means you will have some canes angling off immediately, some going straight up for 2 feet then angling off, some growing straight to 4 feet then angling, and so on. The benefit to this is that each will fill its section of the trellis when you do start to angle it off, because the part going straight up won't produce laterals crowding out the cane beneath it. Instead, it will start producing them at the point you angle it off.

As the canes reach the end of the trellis, gently bend them back toward the opposite edge of the trellis and send them back over and up to the opposite side of the trellis at a 45-degree angle. Once a cane reaches the opposite edge, turn it again and send it back the other way. Each time you snake back and forth across the trellis at a 45-degree angle, you gain height. While a cane is still young and supple, this is easy to do. As a cane gets older and stiffens, it becomes more difficult. So start early.

If a cane at first doesn't want to bend in the opposite direction and be trained at 45 degrees, simply bend it as close to 45 degrees as you can, loosely tie it in place, wait a week or so, and then try again. Quite often, once a rose cane becomes accustomed to a position, it will relax and allow you to bend it further.

Whether you are training your climbing rose on a trellis or some other structure, the principle remains the same. Just try to keep the canes in that horizontal to 45-degree range.

Incorporating climbing roses into your landscape is well worth it. While they require a bit more maintenance than shrub roses, understanding how they grow and bloom will go a long way toward having that wall of roses to sip your cup of tea in front of while perched on a white bench.

VIEW **TRAINING A ROSE ON A TRELLIS** AT WWW.EVERYDAYROSES.COM.

VIEW **COVERING AN ARBOR WITH ROSES** AT WWW.EVERYDAYROSES.COM.

PART 3

Rose Gallery

The Blushing Knock Out rose blending into the landscape.

CHAPTER SIX

Roses in the Landscape

As Peter Beales likes to say, "Don't think of companion plants for roses. Think of roses as companion plants." We traditionally think of how roses grow, and how we grow them, through the prism of the hybrid tea rose. Those "diva" roses take their place in a formal garden in usually the same way. They have an upright growth habit, are all approximately 3 feet by 5 feet in size, and framed by—you guessed it—boxwood!

I want to show you how to use garden roses in the landscape and get them to step out from behind the boxwood. Understand that the analogy of getting out from behind the boxwood is exactly that—an analogy. I have nothing against boxwoods personally. It's what they represent in rose gardening that makes me crazy.

Garden roses come in all shapes and sizes and encompass a broad range of colors. Add in that the vast majority bloom from spring to fall, and you have the most versatile and useful group of true garden plants available.

As you go through this section, don't focus on the particular rose varieties in the photos. (For that, see "Suggested Roses" on p. 148.) Instead, allow yourself to be inspired by how the rose is being used in the garden. Set your roses free from their boxwood enclosure, and let them speak for themselves!

Roses in Flower Borders

Roses have a natural place in any type of flower border. Their range of color, shape, and growth habit can complement a whole host of bulbs, annuals, perennials, and shrubs. Plants with gray-hued foliage and/or flowers of the blue shades are particularly welcome, since those colors are not found in roses. The reason for the latter is that roses lack the gene that produces true blue colors.

Old, spring-flowering roses are extremely well suited for borders. Their early season show outdoes any repeat flowering rose. Then, as the season carries forward, they gracefully step back to provide a green backdrop for summer's perennials and shrubs—including repeat-flowering roses.

Modern garden roses with their continually flowering, brightly colored blooms provide a gardener with a palette of choices rarely seen in other plants. From pinks the color of Bermuda sands to oranges that rival Caribbean sunsets, modern roses in the border are a season-long delight.

Roses had taken their place in borders for hundreds of years before it became the norm to grow them on their own. Today's garden roses are rightfully taking their place among other plants in the garden landscape.

Roses and perennials intermingle freely in a casual garden.

ABOVE: A shrub border in a garden outside Lyon.

BELOW: Knock Out roses complement a garden of mixed flowers.

Roses work well in a border of shrubs.

A traditional English flower border at Mottisfont Abbey in the United Kingdom.

ABOVE: Blues set off the Peach Drift rose blossoms nicely.

BELOW: The Peach Drift works well in a border of shrubs.

Roses in Containers

Many of today's garden roses are being bred to tuck into tighter spaces, as smaller house lots and people's busy lifestyles leave less space and time to tend large garden borders. The added benefit is that many of these roses are also perfectly suitable for growing in containers. On your deck, on your patio, outside the front door, or even in the garden itself as a decorative accent, their use is only limited by the sun's ability to provide them with the direct light they need.

Roses like to spread out their roots, so provide them with a container that allows for depth in their soil environment. It should have a minimum of 18 inches in height and circumference. In it, build a living soil profile exactly as you would in a garden bed (see pp. 31, 44–45 for more information on a living profile). A good potting soil, compost, and beneficial microbes added via a drench will keep your roses healthy and happy.

In containers, the soil gets depleted of nutrients over time, so every few years it's good to replace it. This is best done during pruning time, so as not to shock the rose when it's actively growing. Simply lift the rose out of the pot, dump out the old loose soil, then replace the soil and replant the rose. If the rose's roots are being crowded, this is the time to do some light root pruning so new roots have a place to go (for root-pruning tips, see p. 93).

Lastly, plant other plants in the container. Bulbs and herbs that drape over the side are excellent choices for this.

Growing roses in containers adds an entirely new dimension to your garden; not to mention, it expands the choice of areas to grow them.

Roses in pots make for a very flexible garden.

ABOVE: Rose: 'Mandarin Sunblaze'.

FACING PAGE: Pink Knock Out roses in urns with Rainbow Knock Out roses in the foreground.

The rose 'Lavender Pearl' spills out of a rock border.

Roses as Ground Covers

Today's ground-cover roses offer a wide variety of color for a multitude of uses. They are perfect for the front of a border, since their low-spreading habit hides the knees of the taller plants behind them. Or place them at the top of terrace walls, where their draping habit gracefully breaks up the straight lines of the hardscape.

Consider using them on hillsides for erosion control. As their canes touch the ground, they will frequently set down new roots, and this ever-expanding root network is quite effective in holding the soil during a summer deluge. Certainly, the flowers are a lovelier vista than the commonly used ivy.

Roses are superb in hanging baskets, because they offer ropes of blossoms that tumble out of the container. In large containers with other roses and/or plants, they tumble out and over the edges.

Ground-cover roses have a wide range of uses. How they are used is limited only by the gardener's imagination.

Red Drift roses soften up the edge of a wall.

Roses over Rock Walls

The recent introduction and popularity of ground-cover roses has led to another terrific use for roses: Plant them at the top of a wall and let them naturally spill over the front.

This is particularly useful if you have retaining walls and want to break up their hard horizontal lines. Mix them with other tumbling plants. Herbs particularly come to mind, as they bring the added bonus of scented foliage to mingle with the sweetness of the roses.

When the roses first begin to grow, they will likely grow straight up, but give them time. As their canes lengthen, their weight will pull them down toward the ground. Feel free to coax them forward and over the wall with a little staking, if need be. Once the canes are tumbling, the stakes can be removed.

Roses that naturally tumble over rock walls give all gardeners yet another way of softening some of the hard edges of a garden. And this is yet another way of illustrating how versatile garden roses are.

ABOVE: Rosa filipes 'Kiftsgate' softens the top of a garden wall.

BELOW: Red Drift roses lend to the casual atmosphere of this stone wall.

Red Drift roses frame a set of steps.

Roses as Hedges

Garden roses by definition are excellent choices for hedging because they are well foliated from top to bottom. However, instead of a living wall of constant hue, a rose hedge is bursting with color and texture. Foliage ranges from the gray/green of the Albas to the burgundy hue of the species rose *Rosa rubrifolia* and to the bronze tones of young growth on most roses. Overlay that with flowers of varying shades, sizes, and shapes, and you have a hedge as beautiful as it is practical.

Space the varieties snugly using the same guide discussed in mass planting (see p. 132), and you can even bring them in a little closer to allow their branches to interweave.

An added plus is that rose hedges make good security screens. Seek out varieties dense with wicked, hooked thorns and scatter them liberally throughout the hedge. Many of the old species roses provide a prickly arsenal of deterrents to unwanted intruders. These same thorns offer security for smaller animals and nesting birds. The brightly colored hips of many of the species roses offer a bejeweled winter food source for animals and birds and add winter interest to your garden. It is important to keep in mind that roses are deciduous, so their bare canes will not afford much in the way of privacy screening during the winter months. If you need year-round privacy, you might consider a back row of evergreen plants with roses in front of it.

This combination of form and function make a hedge of roses a head-turning and useful addition to any garden.

Roses bring color to an otherwise purely green hedge.

ABOVE: The 'Queen of Sweden' hedge splits a field of daisies.

BELOW: A hedge of 'The Mayflower' roses frame the back of a flower border.

ABOVE: Twin hedges of The Alnwick® rose draw your eye towards a place of rest.

BELOW: A hedge of Bonica roses frames a water feature.

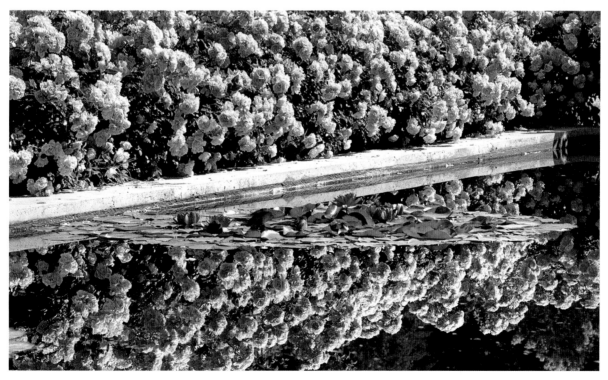

Climbing Roses

Climbing roses are traditionally associated with a rose-covered arbor shading a picket gate at a garden's entrance. They are lovely in that setting, but their uses go well beyond that coffee-table-book vista.

First and foremost, climbing roses add vertical interest to any garden. They literally take gardens to new heights! Think of them on fences, walls, and pergolas. Bring them into the middle of the garden by growing them as pillar roses, on tepee supports, and on any other kind of sculpture you can think of.

As you train them onto their support, keep in mind what we discussed in the care section on climbing roses (see pp. 102–103), which is to keep the main canes between a horizontal orientation and a 45-degree angle in order to produce blooms all along the canes instead of just on the top.

Being able to take a moment in your garden to soak in the warmth of the sun's rays with rose blossoms nodding above you from a climbing rose is something not to be missed. As you seek to create these oasis spots, let your imagination run wild with ways of growing climbing roses.

Climbing Eden™ and White Eden™ grace a pergola.

TOP LEFT: Raspberry Cream Twirl climbs up a pole.

BOTTOM LEFT: Simple structures with climbing roses on them add vertical interest to the garden.

TOP RIGHT: Rambling roses can achieve great size and are a stunning sight in bloom.

BOTTOM RIGHT: Growing climbing roses as pillars allows you to place them almost anywhere in the garden.

A tunnel of climbing roses can draw your eye to other parts of the garden.

A wall of rambling roses in Roseraie de l'Haÿ just south of Paris.

TOP: Roses grow gracefully up a screen in the garden.

BOTTOM RIGHT: Cancan™ gently frames a window.

BOTTOM LEFT: Climbing roses liven up the garden.

Roses in Mass Plantings

A bed of a single rose variety massed together is truly a beautiful sight. The mass of blooms spreads out over the entire bed, making it nearly impossible to see where one single plant ends and the next one begins.

The plants should be planted in close proximity so the edges grow into each other and hide the view of the ground beneath them. To determine spacing, take the rose's suggested mature width and subtract a third. For example, with a suggested width of 3 feet, subtracting one-third (1 foot) leaves a spacing of 2 feet. If you live in a climate warmer than Zone 6 or 7, increase this spacing by about 30 percent to accommodate the fact that roses grow larger in warmer climates.

As mentioned earlier, for the past 50 years, roses were kept far apart from each other to increase air circulation to prevent disease (see "Disease" on pp. 66–70). This was needed for diva roses, but today's garden roses are inherently disease resistant and therefore happy to be planted close to their siblings.

A mass planting of the Knock Out rose subtly transitions to a mass planting of the Pink Knock Out rose.

ABOVE: The rose Bonica provides a focal point in the gardens at Peter Beales Roses.

BELOW: A mass of Knock Out roses.

ABOVE: Mass planted beds in Westbroekpark in The Hague.

BELOW: Sweeping plantings of one variety lend a grand air to Roseraie de l'Haÿ, just south of Paris.

Masses of Various Roses

The only difference between masses of roses and roses in mass planting is that masses of roses are made up of many different rose varieties planted in close proximity to each other. The effect is that of a Persian carpet woven from rose petals floating above waves of green foliage.

Unlike mass planting a bed with only one variety, this type of planting takes some planning. Divide your roses into three height groups: small, medium, and tall. If your bed can only be viewed from the front because of a wall or fence at the back, then the smaller roses go toward the front of the bed, the medium roses go next, and the taller roses are planted toward the back. If your bed is viewable from all sides, the smaller roses rim the edge, the next rim includes the medium growers, and the taller growers make up the center. If they are mixed up, the taller ones can overwhelm the smaller by shading them out or simply blocking your view of them.

To determine spacing, use the same formula as when mass planting one variety (see p. 132), but apply it to each of the three height groups. Generally, each height group will have similar widths; if one doesn't, use your gardener's instincts to add or decrease space around that particular variety. And remember, if it doesn't work, you can always move it next winter.

A beautiful mixture of different types of plantings at Morris Arboretum.

Different colored roses blend well together.

TOP: Roses stretch along a border at Mottisfont Abbey in the United Kingdom.

BOTTOM: A variety of roses adds drama to the garden.

Creative Rose Growing

While we've tried to cover the main ways roses are used in the landscape, don't limit yourself to just these examples. As you continue to discover the versatility of garden roses, let your imagination bring them to new places. We've mentioned several times that garden roses are among the most versatile plants we have in terms of color, growth habit, and size. So if your gardener's instincts whisper to you, "You could probably grow a rose there," then listen to that inner voice. It knows there is indeed the perfect idea and rose for that spot.

A LIVING ARCH

One of the most imaginative rose uses I know is the living arch created by Geertje van der Krogt of Bierkreek Nursery in the Netherlands (see p. 144). She has created an arch from living willow trees to support the classic rambling rose 'Albertine'.

It was inspired by an arch she saw in a nearby city park made of old trees. She thought she could make one in her own garden using a variety of flexible willow that she could grow into the shape and size she wanted. It can be replicated by planting three willows on each side for a total of six, and cutting out all the canes except for one per willow. This leaves three willows close together on each side of the arch, each with one cane. The three canes are gently twisted together as the plant grows. Be sure to not to twist them too tightly, as they must have room to grow and expand. You will have to hold the twists together with string or some other form of soft plant tie that won't cut into the bark. Initially, they will need the support of a stake, but as they mature they become self-supporting, and the stake can be removed. As the willows grow, keep influencing their direction so eventually they meet at the top of what will become your arch.

Geertje's living arch is an example of what happens when creativity meets the versatility of garden roses. The result is beautiful from every aspect!

The 'Frances E. Lester' creates a beautiful shady spot to unwind.

TOP: A living arch blends beautifully into the landscape.

BOTTOM: A rose handrail.

TOP: 'Iceberg' roses frame a path.

BOTTOM: A rose (at right) climbs up a stone arch.

A Living Arch

ABOVE: A living arch in bloom.

BELOW LEFT: It does take more work than a non-living arch!

BELOW CENTER: A close-up of the base after pruning.

BELOW RIGHT: The arch in winter after it—and the rose growing on it—have been pruned.

How about a rose espalier?

PART 4

Rose
Guide

The Sunny Knock Out rose.

Suggested Roses

Following is a list of roses with a brief description of their characteristics and ways they can be used in the landscape (see Chapter 6 for landscape ideas). All respond well to the care techniques discussed in this book. I've put them into groups or "families" (like The Knock Out Family of Roses), because that's a good way to approach purchasing them. Roses within "families" have common characteristics, and my idea here is to introduce you to a few roses from each family. Then you can seek out other roses in the same family that may have a different bloom color, for example.

To also help you in your search, I'm including the International Cultivar Registration Authority for Roses (ICRAR) breeder code. This code helps you determine who bred or created the rose.

The breeder code is generally found right by the name of the rose in a catalog or on the tag on the plant itself. Take, for example, the Knock Out rose. The code is "RADrazz," and the first three to four letters of the code (usually capitalized) indicate the breeder. The breeder of Knock Out is Bill Radler, and R-A-D are the first three letters of his last name. Any code starting with those is a rose bred by Bill. (The "razz" is something Bill or the company introducing the plant made up, and we'll probably never know what it means.) Where appropriate in the descriptions that follow, I've listed the breeder's code so you can use it to spot their roses. For additional help, check the Resources on p. 178.

The Knock Out Family of Roses from Star Roses and Plants/Conard-Pyle

LANDSCAPE USES:

- Borders
- Mass planting
- Masses of roses
- Hedges
- Creative rose growing

Bred by Bill Radler and introduced by Star Roses and Plants/Conard-Pyle, the original Knock Out rose revolutionized the way we think of garden roses in the 21st century. With Knock Out and subsequent members of The Knock Out Family of Roses, gardeners who never before grew roses began adding them to their own landscape. More important, they succeeded and learned that roses are not difficult to grow.

Generally, Knock Out roses grow in a range of 3 to 4 feet wide by 3 to 4 feet high, but in warmer climates and without yearly trimming, many will exceed that. They can be lightly trimmed throughout the season and can even tolerate a very hard prune down to 12 inches. The latter can be done if you need to radically bring them under control from rampant growth or if you wish to rejuvenate the entire plant with new growth for maximum performance.

VARIETY: The Knock Out Rose
ICRAR Code: 'RADrazz'
Bloom Color: Cherry red/hot pink
Zones: 5–11
Height: 3–4 feet
Width: 3–4 feet
Fragrance: None (though a light tea fragrance can be noted in some conditions)
Flowering: Flowers from spring to first hard frost, every 5–6 weeks
Growth Habit: Compact, mounding, bushy growth
Foliage: Purple on young leaves maturing to dark green
Bloom Type: Single
Light Conditions: Full sun

VARIETY: The Double Knock Out Rose
ICRAR Code: 'RADtko'
Bloom Color: Cherry red
Zones: 5–11
Height: 3–4 feet
Width: 3–4 feet
Fragrance: None (though a light tea fragrance can be noted in some conditions)
Flowering: Flowers from spring to first hard frost, every 5–6 weeks
Growth Habit: Compact, mounding, bushy growth
Foliage: Purple on young leaves maturing to dark green
Bloom Type: Double
Light Conditions: Full sun

The Double Knock Out Rose

VARIETY: The Pink Knock Out Rose
ICRAR Code: 'RADcon'
Bloom Color: Bright pink
Zones: 5–11
Height: 3–4 feet
Width: 3–4 feet
Fragrance: None (though a light tea fragrance can be noted in some conditions)
Flowering: Flowers from spring to first hard frost, every 5–6 weeks
Growth Habit: Bushy, mounding growth
Foliage: Dark green
Bloom Type: Single
Light Conditions: Full sun

VARIETY: The Pink Double Knock Out Rose
ICRAR Code: 'RADtkopink'
Bloom Color: Pink
Zones: 5–11
Height: 3–4 feet
Width: 3–4 feet
Fragrance: None (though a light tea fragrance can be noted in some conditions)
Flowering: Flowers from spring to first hard frost, every 5–6 weeks
Growth Habit: Compact, mounding, bushy growth
Foliage: Dark green
Bloom Type: Double
Light Conditions: Full sun

The Pink Double Knock Out Rose

VARIETY: The Sunny Knock Out Rose
ICRAR Code: 'RADsunny'
Bloom Color: Yellow, cream/white
Zones: 5–11
Height: 3–4 feet
Width: 3–4 feet
Fragrance: Sweetbriar
Flowering: Flowers from spring to first hard frost, every 5–6 weeks
Growth Habit: Upright growth
Foliage: Dark green
Bloom Type: Single
Light Conditions: Full sun

The Sunny Knock Out Rose

Drift Ground-cover Roses from Star Roses and Plants/ Conard-Pyle

LANDSCAPE USES:

- Borders
- Ground covers
- Containers
- Mass planting
- Masses of roses
- Roses over walls
- Creative rose growing

Also introduced by Star Roses and Plants/Conard-Pyle and bred by the venerable nursery of Meilland® International (breeder code MEI) in France, this is an excellent line of roses for smaller gardens. Like The Knock Out Family of Roses, they are repeat flowering, disease resistant, and virtually maintenance free.

They are a cross between full-size ground-cover roses and miniature roses. From the former, they gain their toughness, disease resistance, and winter hardiness. From the miniatures, they inherit their well-mannered size and repeat-blooming nature.

The sizes range from 2 to 3 feet wide to 1 to 2 feet tall. They have a low-spreading growth habit. You can trim them lightly all year or prune hard in early spring for maximum performance.

VARIETY: Popcorn Drift
ICRAR Code: 'NOVarospop'
Bloom Color: Cream yellow, finish pure white
Zones: 5–11
Height: 1–2 feet
Width: 2 feet
Fragrance: None

Flowering: Flowers from spring to first hard frost, every 5–6 weeks
Growth Habit: Ground cover, bushy growth
Foliage: Medium green
Bloom Type: Double
Light Conditions: Full sun

Popcorn Drift

VARIETY: Apricot Drift
ICRAR Code: 'MEImirrote'
Bloom Color: Apricot
Zones: 4–11
Height: 1–2 feet
Width: 2–3 feet
Fragrance: None
Flowering: Flowers from spring to first hard frost, every 5–6 weeks
Growth Habit: Ground cover, bushy growth
Foliage: Dark green
Bloom Type: Fully double
Light Conditions: Full sun

Apricot Drift

VARIETY: Coral Drift
ICRAR Code: 'MEIdrifora'
Bloom Color: Coral
Zones: 4–11
Height: 1–2 feet
Width: 2–3 feet
Fragrance: None (though a light apple fragrance can be noted in some conditions)

Flowering: Flowers from spring to first hard frost, every 5–6 weeks
Growth Habit: Ground cover, bushy growth
Foliage: Dark green
Bloom Type: Semi-double
Light Conditions: Full sun

VARIETY: Peach Drift
ICRAR Code: 'MEIggili'
Bloom Color: Peach
Zones: 4–11
Height: 1–2 feet
Width: 2 feet
Fragrance: None
Flowering: Flowers from spring to first hard frost, every 5–6 weeks
Growth Habit: Ground cover, bushy growth
Foliage: Dark green
Bloom Type: Double
Light Conditions: Full sun

VARIETY: Pink Drift
ICRAR Code: 'MEIjocos'
Bloom Color: Pink
Zones: 4–11
Height: 1–2 feet
Width: 3 feet
Fragrance: None
Flowering: Flowers from spring to first hard frost, every 5–6 weeks
Growth Habit: Ground cover, bushy, creeping growth
Foliage: Dark green
Bloom Type: Single
Light Conditions: Full sun

Pink Drift

VARIETY: Red Drift
ICRAR Code: 'MEIgalpio'
Bloom Color: Red
Zones: 4–11
Height: 1–2 feet
Width: 2–3 feet
Fragrance: None

Flowering: Flowers from spring to first hard frost, every 5–6 weeks
Growth Habit: Ground cover, bushy, creeping growth
Foliage: Dark green
Bloom Type: Semi-double
Light Conditions: Full sun

VARIETY: Sweet Drift
ICRAR Code: 'MEIswetdom'
Bloom Color: Pink to light pink
Zone: 4–11
Height: 1–2 feet
Width: 2–3 feet
Fragrance: None
Flowering: Flowers from spring to first hard frost, every 5–6 weeks
Growth Habit: Ground cover, bushy growth
Foliage: Dark green
Bloom Type: Fully double
Light Conditions: Full sun

Carefree Landscape Roses from Star Roses and Plants/Conard-Pyle

LANDSCAPE USES:
- Borders
- Containers (some varieties)
- Mass planting
- Masses of roses
- Creative rose growing

Carefree Landscape Roses are a newer series from Star Roses and Plants/Conard-Pyle that include a diversity of growth habits, so it's best to evaluate each one individually in terms of garden use. That being said, most are in the short to medium height range of about 3 to 5 feet. They also are disease resistant and easy to care for.

Growth habit ranges from compact to spreading, making them suitable for a variety of uses.

VARIETY: Carefree Delight™
ICRAR Code: 'MEIpotal'
Bloom Color: Pink with white center
Zones: 5–9
Height: 3–5 feet
Width: 3½–4 feet
Fragrance: None
Flowering: Flowers from spring to fall
Growth Habit: Bushy, tall upright growth
Foliage: Medium green
Bloom Type: Single
Light Conditions: Full sun

VARIETY: Carefree Spirit™
ICRAR Code: 'MEIzmea'
Bloom Color: Deep cherry red with white center
Zones: 5–9
Height: 5 feet
Width: 5 feet
Fragrance: None to slight fragrance
Flowering: Flowers from spring to fall
Growth Habit: Bushy, mounding growth
Foliage: Dark green
Bloom Type: Single
Light Conditions: Full sun

Carefree Spirit

VARIETY: Carefree Sunshine™
ICRAR Code: 'RADsun'
Bloom Color: Light yellow
Zones: 5–9
Height: 4½–5 feet
Width: 3–4 feet
Fragrance: None
Flowering: Flowers from spring to fall
Growth Habit: Bushy, tall upright growth
Foliage: Medium green
Bloom Type: Semi-double
Light Conditions: Full sun

VARIETY: Carefree Wonder™
ICRAR Code: 'MEIpitac'
Bloom Color: Bright pink
Zones: 5–9

Height: 3–4 feet
Width: 3–4 feet
Fragrance: Mild fragrance
Flowering: Flowers from spring to fall
Growth Habit: Bushy, tall upright growth
Foliage: Medium green
Bloom Type: Double
Light Conditions: Full sun

Meidiland® Landscape Roses from Star Roses and Plants/Conard-Pyle

LANDSCAPE USES:
- Borders
- Containers
- Mass planting
- Masses of roses
- Roses over rock walls
- Creative rose growing

Meidiland (breeder code MEI, also from Meilland International) Landscape Roses have a graceful, loose, and spreading growth habit. Their average size is 3 feet by 3 feet. They bloom from spring to fall and are available in a wide range of colors. Care is minimal, and as they mature, they will reward gardeners with clouds of blooms above dark green foliage.

VARIETY: Fire Meidiland
ICRAR Code: 'MEIpsidue'
Bloom Color: Bright red
Zones: 5–9
Height: 1–2 feet
Width: 4–5 feet
Fragrance: None
Flowering: Flowers from spring to fall
Growth Habit: Bushy, mounding growth
Foliage: Medium green
Bloom Type: Double
Light Conditions: Full sun

VARIETY: Crimson Meidiland
ICRAR Code: 'MEIzerbil'
Bloom Color: Bright red
Zones: 5–9
Height: 2 feet
Width: 4 feet
Fragrance: None
Flowering: Flowers from spring to fall
Growth Habit: Bushy, mounding growth
Foliage: Dark green
Bloom Type: Semi-double
Light Conditions: Full sun

Crimson Meidiland

VARIETY: Fairy Meidiland
ICRAR Code: 'MEIklutz'
Bloom Color: Carmine pink
Zones: 5–9
Height: 3 feet
Width: 3 feet
Fragrance: None to slight fragrance
Flowering: Flowers from spring to fall
Growth Habit: Bushy, tall upright growth
Foliage: Dark green
Bloom Type: Semi-double
Light Conditions: Full sun

Fairy Meidiland

VARIETY: Lavender Meidiland
ICRAR Code: 'MEIbivers'
Bloom Color: Deep pink with lavender reverse
Zones: 5–9

Height: 3–4 feet
Width: 3–4 feet
Fragrance: Mild fragrance
Flowering: Flowers from spring to fall
Growth Habit: Mounding growth
Foliage: Medium green
Bloom Type: Double
Light Conditions: Full sun

Lavender Meidiland

Romantica® Roses from Star Roses and Plants/Conard-Pyle

LANDSCAPE USES:

- Borders (excluding climbers)
- Mass planting (excluding climbers)
- Masses of roses (excluding climbers)
- Climbing roses (only climbers)
- Screens (only climbers)
- Creative rose growing

This collection couples old-fashioned cupped-style blooms with today's modern disease resistance. The growth habits vary widely, so evaluate each one individually for garden use. Some are even climbers.

Some of the larger-growing varieties need a season or two to get established before they truly come into their own, so be patient if a particular variety doesn't

perform to your expectations in the first year. Care is minimal.

VARIETY: Traviata™
ICRAR Code: 'MEIlavio'
Bloom Color: Dark red
Zones: 6–9
Height: 3–4 feet
Width: 4–5 feet
Fragrance: Slight
Flowering: Flowers from spring to fall
Growth Habit: Bushy, tall upright growth
Foliage: Dark green
Bloom Type: Fully double
Light Conditions: Full sun

Traviata

VARIETY: Pink Traviata
ICRAR Code: 'MEItravia'
Bloom Color: Deep pink
Zones: 6–9
Height: 3–4 feet
Width: 4–5 feet
Fragrance: Slight
Flowering: Flowers from spring to fall
Growth Habit: Tall/upright growth
Foliage: Dark green
Bloom Type: Fully double
Light Conditions: Full sun

VARIETY: Abbaye de Cluny™
ICRAR Code: 'MEIbrinpay'
Bloom Color: Soft apricot
Zones: 5–9
Height: 3–4 feet
Width: 3–4 feet
Fragrance: Moderate, spicy citrus
Flowering: Flowers from spring to fall
Growth Habit: Bushy growth
Foliage: Dark green
Bloom Type: Fully double
Light Conditions: Full sun

VARIETY: Jean Giono™
ICRAR Code: 'MEIrokoi'
Bloom Color: Golden yellow
Zones: 5–9

Height: 2–3 feet
Width: 2–3 feet
Fragrance: Moderate spice
Flowering: Flowers from spring to fall
Growth Habit: Bushy growth
Foliage: Dark green
Bloom Type: Fully double
Light Conditions: Full sun

VARIETY: Orchid Romance™
ICRAR Code: 'RADprov'
Bloom Color: Medium pink to lavender
Zones: 6–9
Height: 4–5 feet
Width: 3 feet
Fragrance: Strong, citrusy
Flowering: Flowers from spring to fall
Growth Habit: Bushy, upright growth
Foliage: Dark green
Bloom Type: Fully double
Light Conditions: Full sun

Orchid Romance

VARIETY: Eden Climber™
ICRAR Code: 'MEIviolin'
Bloom Color: Pink edged in white
Zones: 5–9
Height: 10–12 feet
Width: N/A
Fragrance: Slight
Flowering: Flowers from spring to fall
Growth Habit: Climbing rose
Foliage: Dark green
Bloom Type: Fully double
Light Conditions: Full sun

VARIETY: Bolero™
ICRAR Code: 'MEIdeweis'
Bloom Color: White
Zones: 5–9
Height: 3–4 feet
Width: 3–4 feet
Fragrance: Old rose and spice
Flowering: Flowers from spring to fall
Growth Habit: Bushy growth
Foliage: Dark green

Bloom Type: Fully double
Light Conditions: Full sun

Bolero

Hardy Climbers from Star Roses and Plants/ Conard-Pyle

LANDSCAPE USES:
- **Climbing roses**
- **Screens**

A relatively new line of roses from Star Roses and Plants/Conard-Pyle, the Hardy Climbers were bred by Bill Radler, who gave us The Knock Out Family of Roses. This is a series of repeat-flowering climbers that are all winter hardy.

These climbers are a significant addition to the world of garden roses because while there is a broad range of repeat-flowering climbing roses, most of them are hardy only to Zone 6. So finding disease-resistant, repeat-flowering climbing roses hardy to Zone 5 is not easy, which makes this a welcome collection.

The roses are modest in size to about 10 feet, and all respond to the methods of growing climbing roses discussed in this book.

VARIETY: Winners Circle™
ICRAR Code: 'RADwin'
Bloom Color: Bright red
Zones: 5–9
Height: 10–12 feet
Width: N/A
Fragrance: None
Flowering: Flowers from spring to fall
Growth Habit: Climbing rose
Foliage: Dark green
Bloom Type: Single
Light Conditions: Full sun

VARIETY: Morning Magic™
ICRAR Code: 'RADmor'
Bloom Color: Shell pink
Zones: 5–9
Height: 7–8 feet
Width: N/A
Fragrance: None
Flowering: Flowers from spring to fall
Growth Habit: Climbing rose
Foliage: Dark green
Bloom Type: Semi-double
Light Conditions: Full sun

Morning Magic

VARIETY: Brite Eyes™
ICRAR Code: 'RADbrite'
Bloom Color: Salmon pink
Zones: 5–9
Height: 7–8 feet
Width: N/A
Fragrance: Mild spicy

Brite Eyes

Flowering: Flowers from spring to fall
Growth Habit: Climbing rose
Foliage: Medium green
Bloom Type: Single
Light Conditions: Full sun

VARIETY: Cancan
ICRAR Code: 'RADcancan'
Bloom Color: Magenta red to light pink
Zones: 5–9
Height: 10 feet
Width: N/A
Fragrance: None
Flowering: Flowers from spring to fall
Growth Habit: Climbing rose
Foliage: Medium green
Bloom Type: Double
Light Conditions: Full sun

Cancan

Oso Easy® and Oso Happy™ Series from Spring Meadow Nursery

LANDSCAPE USES:

- Borders
- Containers
- Ground covers (spreading varieties)
- Mass planting
- Masses of roses
- Roses over rock walls (spreading varieties)
- Creative rose growing

Part of the Proven Winners® brand from Spring Meadow, this group of garden roses comprises disease-resistant roses. Their growth habit is mostly short and compact, but there are some spreading roses in the series that are useful as ground cover or to use tumbling over rock walls.

The series contains a broad range of color and blooms. They can be lightly trimmed during the seasons, but if needed, an occasional hard prune will keep them in check.

VARIETY: Oso Happy Smoothie
ICRAR Code: 'ZLEsak Poly3'
Bloom Color: Hot pink
Zones: 4–9
Height: 3 feet
Width: 3 feet
Fragrance: None
Flowering: Flowers from spring to fall
Growth Habit: Mounding growth, thornless
Foliage: Medium green
Bloom Type: Single
Light Conditions: Full sun

Oso Happy Smoothie

VARIETY: Oso Happy Petit Pink
ICRAR Code: 'ZLEMarianneYoshida'
Bloom Color: Medium pink
Zones: 4–9
Height: 3–4 feet high
Width: 3–4 feet wide
Fragrance: None
Flowering: Flowers from spring to fall
Growth Habit: Mounding, spreading growth
Foliage: Medium green
Bloom Type: Double
Light Conditions: Full sun

VARIETY: Oso Easy Cherry Pie
ICRAR Code: 'MEIboulka'
Bloom Color: Candy apple red
Zones: 4–9
Height: 2–4 feet
Width: 2–4 feet

Fragrance: None
Flowering: Flowers from spring to fall
Growth Habit: Mounding, spreading growth
Foliage: Medium green
Bloom Type: Single
Light Conditions: Full sun

VARIETY: Oso Easy Mango Salsa
ICRAR Code: 'CHEWperAdventure'
Bloom Color: Ruby red
Zones: 4–9
Height: 2–3 feet
Width: 2–3 feet
Fragrance: None
Flowering: Flowers from spring to fall
Growth Habit: Mounding growth
Foliage: Dark green
Bloom Type: Double
Light Conditions: Full sun

Oso Easy Mango Salsa

VARIETY: Oso Happy Candy Oh!
ICRAR Code: 'ZLEMatinCipar'
Bloom Color: Candy apple red
Zones: 4–9
Height: 3–4 feet
Width: 3–4 feet
Fragrance: None
Flowering: Flowers from spring to fall
Growth Habit: Mounding growth
Foliage: Medium green
Bloom Type: Single
Light Conditions: Full sun

VARIETY: Oso Easy Peachy Cream
ICRAR Code: 'HORcoherent'
Bloom Color: Peach fading to cream
Zones: 4–9
Height: 1–3 feet
Width: 1–3 feet
Fragrance: None
Flowering: Flowers from spring to fall
Growth Habit: Mounding growth

Foliage: Dark green
Bloom Type: Semi-double
Light Conditions: Full sun

VARIETY: Oso Easy Paprika
ICRAR Code: 'CHEWmaytime'
Bloom Color: Bright orange
Zones: 4–9
Height: 1–2 feet
Width: 2–3 feet
Fragrance: None
Flowering: Flowers from spring to fall
Growth Habit: Mounding, spreading growth
Foliage: Dark green
Bloom Type: Semi-double
Light Conditions: Full sun

Oso Easy Paprika

Easy Elegance from Bailey Nurseries

LANDSCAPE USES:

- Borders
- Containers (the shorter varieties)
- Mass planting
- Masses of roses
- Roses as hedges (for smaller hedges)
- Creative rose growing

The Easy Elegance Rose Collection from Bailey Nurseries is a series of shrub roses bred by Ping Lim. They were registered under Bailey Nurseries, which is why the code does not reflect his name. (If you want to find all the Bailey roses specific to Ping Lim, you can look them up on www.helpmefind.com/roses.)

Their sizes range from 2 to 4 feet with a few reaching 5 feet. Compact in nature, they offer a broad range of color and bloom shape coupled with excellent disease resistance and hardiness.

VARIETY: Music Box
ICRAR Code: 'BALbox'
Bloom Color: Creamy yellow center surrounded by soft pink
Zones: 4–9
Height: 3 feet
Width: 3 feet
Fragrance: None
Flowering: Flowers from spring to fall
Growth Habit: Mounding growth
Foliage: Medium green
Bloom Type: Double
Light Conditions: Full sun

VARIETY: Sunrise Sunset
ICRAR Code: 'BALset'
Bloom Color: Fuchsia with apricot centers
Zones: 4–9
Height: 2–3 feet
Width: 3–4 feet
Fragrance: None
Flowering: Flowers from spring to fall
Growth Habit: Mounding, spreading growth
Foliage: Medium green
Bloom Type: Double
Light Conditions: Full sun

Sunrise Sunset

VARIETY: Macy's Pride
ICRAR Code: 'BALcream'
Bloom Color: Lemon yellow
Zones: 4–9
Height: 3–5 feet
Width: 2–3 feet
Fragrance: None

Flowering: Flowers from spring to fall
Growth Habit: Bushy, upright growth
Foliage: Purple on young leaves maturing to dark green
Bloom Type: Double
Light Conditions: Full sun

VARIETY: All the Rage
ICRAR Code: 'BALrage'
Bloom Color: Coral apricot with yellow center
Zones: 4–9
Height: 3–4 feet
Width: 2–3 feet
Fragrance: None
Flowering: Flowers from spring to fall
Growth Habit: Bushy, mounding growth
Foliage: Medium green
Bloom Type: Semi-double
Light Conditions: Full sun

All the Rage

VARIETY: My Girl
ICRAR Code: 'BALgirl'
Bloom Color: Deep Pink
Zones: 4–9
Height: 3–4 feet
Width: 3–4 feet
Fragrance: None
Flowering: Flowers from spring to fall
Growth Habit: Bushy, mounding growth
Foliage: Medium green
Bloom Type: Double
Light Conditions: Full sun

VARIETY: Kashmir
ICRAR Code: 'BALmir'
Bloom Color: Velvety Red
Zones: 4–9
Height: 3–4 feet
Width: 2–3 feet
Fragrance: None
Flowering: Flowers from spring to fall

Growth Habit: Bushy, upright growth
Foliage: Medium green
Bloom Type: Fully double
Light Conditions: Full sun

Kashmir

Biltmore Garden Rose Collection by Biltmore for Your Home

LANDSCAPE USES:

- Borders (excluding climbers)
- Containers (shorter growing varieties)
- Roses in mass planting (excluding climbers)
- Masses of roses (excluding climbers)
- Climbing roses
- Roses as hedges (taller varieties)
- Roses as screens
- Creative rose growing

This relatively new collection is being assembled from garden roses all over the world that are currently not offered in North America. A multitude of rose breeders are contributing roses in a range of growth habits, sizes, and colors.

The common themes among them are disease resistance, fragrance, and ease of care. Because of this, each variety should be individually evaluated for its garden use. The collection offers a range of carefree roses in a variety of colors and sizes.

VARIETY: Flamenco Rosita
ICRAR Code: 'BEAdonald'
Bloom Color: Cherry red
Zones: 5–9
Height: 5 feet
Width: 6 feet
Fragrance: Mild fragrance
Flowering: Flowers from spring to fall
Growth Habit: Tall, spreading growth
Foliage: Dark green
Bloom Type: Fully double
Light Conditions: Full sun

Flamenco

VARIETY: Southern Peach
ICRAR Code: 'JAPgoldie'
Bloom Color: Apricot yellow
Zones: 5–9
Height: 2–3 feet
Width: 2 feet
Fragrance: Moderate, spicy fragrance
Flowering: Flowers from spring to fall
Growth Habit: Upright growth
Foliage: Dark green
Bloom Type: Fully double
Light Conditions: Full sun

VARIETY: Lady Ashe
ICRAR Code: 'BEAdix'
Bloom Color: Apricot salmon
Zones: 5–9
Height: 10–12 feet
Width: N/A
Fragrance: Strong fragrance
Flowering: Flowers from spring to fall
Growth Habit: Climbing rose
Foliage: Dark green
Bloom Type: Fully double
Light Conditions: Full sun

VARIETY: Smart & Sassy
(aka 'Paula Smart')
ICRAR Code: 'JALbrilliant'
Bloom Color: Satin red with golden reverse
Zones: 5–9
Height: 2–3 feet
Width: 2 feet
Fragrance: Moderate fragrance
Flowering: Flowers from spring to fall
Growth Habit: Upright growth
Foliage: Dark green
Bloom Type: Fully double
Light Conditions: Full sun

Smart & Sassy

VARIETY: Loretta Lynn Van Lear
ICRAR Code: 'JALpeach'
Bloom Color: Apricot peach
Zones: 5–9
Height: 2–3 feet
Width: 2–3 feet
Fragrance: Light fragrance
Flowering: Flowers from spring to fall
Growth Habit: Bushy, mounding growth
Foliage: Medium green
Bloom Type: Fully double
Light Conditions: Full sun

Loretta Lynn Van Lear

Delbard Family of Garden Roses Licensed by Paul Zimmerman Roses

LANDSCAPE USES:

- Borders (excluding climbers)
- Containers (shorter varieties)
- Mass planting (excluding climbers)
- Masses of roses (excluding climbers)
- Climbing roses
- Climbing roses as screens
- Creative rose growing

The French nursery of Delbard (breeder code DEL) has been breeding roses for more than 75 years. The nursery started when the founder, Georges Delbard, starting selling plants from a cart in the streets of Paris.

Their growth habits range from compact shrubs to climbers, so each variety should be evaluated individually for garden use. The roses with larger blooms have a very nice fragrance, and among the Painter Series of roses, some very colorful varieties can be found.

VARIETY: Nahema
ICRAR Code: 'DELeri'
Bloom Color: Soft pink
Zones: 5–9
Height: 10–12 feet
Width: N/A
Fragrance: Strong fragrance
Flowering: Flowers from spring to fall
Growth Habit: Climbing rose
Foliage: Medium green
Bloom Type: Fully double
Light Conditions: Full sun

VARIETY: Dames de Chenonceau
ICRAR Code: 'DELpabra'
Bloom Color: Medium pink
Zones: 5–9
Height: 3–5 feet
Width: 3–4 feet
Fragrance: Strong fragrance
Flowering: Flowers from spring to fall
Growth Habit: Bushy growth
Foliage: Dark green
Bloom Type: Fully double
Light Conditions: Full sun

Dames de Chenonceau

VARIETY: Alfred Sisley
ICRAR Code: 'DELstrijor'
Bloom Color: Orange streaked with white
Zones: 5–9
Height: 3–4 feet
Width: 2–3 feet
Fragrance: Mild fragrance
Flowering: Flowers from spring to fall
Growth Habit: Bushy, upright growth
Foliage: Dark green
Bloom Type: Double
Light Conditions: Full sun

Alfred Sisley

VARIETY: Henri Matisse
ICRAR Code: 'DELstrobia'
Bloom Color: Red with deep pink and white stripes
Zones: 5–9
Height: 4–5 feet
Width: 3–4 feet
Fragrance: Mild fragrance
Flowering: Flowers from spring to fall

Growth Habit: Bushy, upright growth
Foliage: Dark green
Bloom Type: Double
Light Conditions: Full sun

VARIETY: Bordure Nacree
ICRAR Code: 'DELcrouf'
Bloom Color: Soft apricot yellow
Zones: 5–9
Height: 2–3 feet
Width: 2–3 feet
Fragrance: None to slight fragrance
Flowering: Flowers from spring to fall
Growth Habit: Bushy, mounding growth
Foliage: Medium green
Bloom Type: Double
Light Conditions: Full sun

Bordure Nacree

VARIETY: Le Rouge et le Noir
ICRAR Code: 'DELcart'
Bloom Color: Deep red
Zones: 5–9
Height: 4–5 feet
Width: 2–3 feet
Fragrance: Strong fragrance
Flowering: Flowers from spring to fall
Growth Habit: Upright growth
Foliage: Dark green
Bloom Type: Fully double
Light Conditions: Full sun

VARIETY: Mme. Figaro
ICRAR Code: 'DELrona'
Bloom Color: Soft pink to white
Zones: 5–9
Height: 4–5 feet
Width: 2–3 feet
Fragrance: Strong fragrance
Flowering: Flowers from spring to fall
Growth Habit: Upright growth
Foliage: Dark green
Bloom Type: Fully double
Light Conditions: Full sun

Weeks Roses by Tom Carruth

LANDSCAPE USES:

- Flower borders (excluding climbers)
- Containers (the shorter shrubs)
- Mass planting (excluding climbers)
- Masses of roses (excluding climbers)
- Climbing roses (climbers and some taller shrubs)
- Roses as hedges (taller shrubs)
- Climbing roses as screens
- Creative rose growing

For many years, Tom Carruth was the rose breeder for Weeks Roses, a wholesale rose nursery that was based in California. His roses were registered under Weeks Roses, so he does not have a specific code to his name. (For additional Weeks Roses specific to Tom Carruth, you can look them up on www.helpmefind.com/roses.) Tom retired from Weeks in 2012, but his roses live on.

His range of roses is broad, from shrubs to climbers, so evaluate each one individually for garden use. All respond nicely to good garden maintenance and bloom from spring to fall. Some of the larger shrubs make excellent climbers in warmer climates.

VARIETY: Cinco de Mayo
ICRAR Code: 'WEKcobeju'
Bloom Color: Smoked lavender and rusty red/orange
Zones: 5–9
Height: 3–5 feet
Width: 3–4 feet
Fragrance: Moderate sweet apple fragrance
Flowering: Flowers from spring to fall
Growth Habit: Bushy, rounded growth
Foliage: Medium green
Bloom Type: Double
Light Conditions: Full sun

VARIETY: Julia Child
ICRAR Code: 'WEKvossutono'
Bloom Color: Butter gold
Zones: 5–9
Height: 3–5 feet
Width: 2–3 feet
Fragrance: Strong licorice candy fragrance
Flowering: Flowers from spring to fall
Growth Habit: Bushy, rounded growth
Foliage: Medium green
Bloom Type: Fully double
Light Conditions: Full sun

Julia Child

VARIETY: Purple Splash
ICRAR Code: 'WEKspitrib'
Bloom Color: Purple with lavender stripes
Zones: 5–9
Height: 10–12 feet high
Width: N/A
Fragrance: Moderate sweet apple fragrance
Flowering: Flowers from spring to fall
Growth Habit: Climbing rose
Foliage: Bright green
Bloom Type: Semi-double
Light Conditions: Full sun

Purple Splash

VARIETY: Ruby Ruby
ICRAR Code: 'WEKsactrumi'
Bloom Color: Cherry red
Zones: 5–9
Height: 1–2 feet
Width: 1–2 feet
Fragrance: Slight fragrance
Flowering: Flowers from spring to fall
Growth Habit: Bushy, rounded growth
Foliage: Dark green
Bloom Type: Fully double
Light Conditions: Full sun

VARIETY: Memorial Day
ICRAR Code: 'WEKblunez
Bloom Color: Orchid pink'
Zones: 5–9
Height: 4–5 feet
Width: 2–3 feet
Fragrance: Strong fragrance
Flowering: Flowers from spring to fall
Growth Habit: Upright growth
Foliage: Medium green
Bloom Type: Fully double
Light Conditions: Full sun

Memorial Day

Polyantha Family of Roses

LANDSCAPE USES:

- Borders
- Containers
- Mass plantings
- Masses of roses
- Hedges (short hedges)
- Roses over rock walls
- Creative rose growing

Polyantha is a class rose, almost all of which make excellent garden roses. Perhaps the most well-known polyantha is a rose called 'The Fairy'. As a group, they stay in the 3- to 5-feet range and bear clusters of smaller blooms on short stems.

Polyantha roses take well to trimming and shaping all season long. They are excellent for use on rock walls; though they don't tumble, their bottom branches will spill slightly over the edge. There are few climbing polyantha roses, so be aware of that as you shop for them. Their versatility and color make them welcome additions to the garden.

VARIETY: Marjorie Fair®
ICRAR Code: 'HARHero'
Bloom Color: Bright red
Zones: 5–10
Height: 3–5 feet
Width: 3–4 feet
Fragrance: Slight fragrance
Flowering: Flowers from spring to fall
Growth Habit: Bushy, spreading growth
Foliage: Light green
Bloom Type: Single
Light Conditions: Full sun/dappled light

Marjorie Fair

VARIETY: 'Mlle. Cecile Brunner'
ICRAR Code: None
Bloom Color: Soft pink
Zones: 5–9
Height: 3–5 feet
Width: 3–4 feet
Fragrance: Moderate fragrance
Flowering: Flowers from spring to fall
Growth Habit: Bushy, upright growth

Foliage: Dark green
Bloom Type: Double
Light Conditions: Full sun

VARIETY: 'Perle d'Or'
ICRAR Code: None
Bloom Color: Apricot yellow
Zones: 6–9
Height: 4–6 feet
Width: 3–4 feet
Fragrance: Moderate fragrance
Flowering: Flowers from spring to fall
Growth Habit: Bushy, upright growth
Foliage: Medium green
Bloom Type: Double
Light Conditions: Full sun

VARIETY: 'Marie Pavie'
ICRAR Code: None
Bloom Color: White
Zones: 5–9
Height: 2–4 feet
Width: 2–3 feet
Fragrance: Moderate fragrance
Flowering: Flowers from spring to fall
Growth Habit: Bushy, rounded growth
Foliage: Dark green
Bloom Type: Double
Light Conditions: Full sun

VARIETY: 'Margo Koster'
ICRAR Code: None
Bloom Color: Salmon orange
Zones: 5–10
Height: 2–4 feet
Width: 2–3 feet
Fragrance: Slight fragrance
Flowering: Flowers from spring to fall
Growth Habit: Bushy, rounded growth
Foliage: Dark green
Bloom Type: Double
Light Conditions: Full sun

'Margo Koster'

VARIETY: 'The Fairy'
ICRAR Code: None
Bloom Color: Medium pink
Zones: 5–9
Height: 2–4 feet
Width: 4–5 feet
Fragrance: Slight fragrance
Flowering: Flowers from spring to fall
Growth Habit: Bushy, rounded growth
Foliage: Dark green
Bloom Type: Double
Light Conditions: Full sun

'The Fairy'

Hybrid Musk Family of Roses

LANDSCAPE USES:
- Borders
- Mass planting
- Masses of roses
- Creative rose growing

Hybrid musk is another class of roses that are very useful in the garden. They have a nice color variety, and they are almost all disease resistant. What's more, they can tolerate a little less sunlight than other roses.

Hybrid musk roses were originally created by the Rev. Joseph Pemberton in the early part of the last century, but some breeders, like Paul Barden, have continued to breed new ones. As they mature, they make mounding shrubs up to 6 feet tall and 6 feet wide. In warmer climates, some can be grown as short climbers on a pillar or low fence. Some are fragrant, and all are easy to grow and give little fuss in the garden.

VARIETY: 'Buff Beauty'
ICRAR Code: None
Bloom Color: Apricot yellow
Zones: 5b–10b
Height: 5–8 feet
Width: 4–6 feet
Fragrance: Strong fragrance
Flowering: Flowers from spring to fall
Growth Habit: Bushy, spreading growth
Foliage: Medium green
Bloom Type: Fully double
Light Conditions: Full sun/dappled light

'Buff Beauty'

VARIETY: 'Darlow's Enigma'
ICRAR Code: None
Bloom Color: White
Zones: 4b–10b
Height: 6–12 feet
Width: 6–8 feet
Fragrance: Strong fragrance
Flowering: Flowers from spring to fall
Growth Habit: Bushy, spreading growth
Foliage: Dark green
Bloom Type: Semi-double
Light Conditions: Full sun/dappled light

VARIETY: 'Daybreak'
ICRAR Code: None
Bloom Color: Medium yellow
Zones: 6b–10b
Height: 4–5 feet
Width: 3–4 feet
Fragrance: Moderate fragrance
Flowering: Flowers from spring to fall
Growth Habit: Bushy, spreading growth
Foliage: Purple on young leaves maturing to dark green

Bloom Type: Double
Light Conditions: Full sun, can take dappled light

VARIETY: 'Prosperity'
ICRAR Code: None
Bloom Color: White
Zones: 6b–10b
Height: 5–8 feet
Width: 4–6 feet
Fragrance: Moderate fragrance
Flowering: Flowers from spring to fall
Growth Habit: Bushy, spreading growth
Foliage: Dark green
Bloom Type: Fully double
Light Conditions: Full sun, can take dappled light

'Prosperity'

VARIETY: 'Wilhelm'
ICRAR Code: None
Bloom Color: Dark red
Zones: 6b–10b
Height: 6–8 feet
Width: 5–6 feet
Fragrance: Moderate honey fragrance
Flowering: Flowers from spring to fall
Growth Habit: Bushy, spreading growth habit; also short climber in warm climates
Foliage: Medium green
Bloom Type: Semi-double
Light Conditions: Full sun/dappled light

'Wilhelm'

Tea Family of Roses

LANDSCAPE USES:
- **Roses in flower borders**
- **Roses in mass planting**
- **Masses of roses**
- **Roses as hedges**
- **Creative rose growing**

Tea is a class of roses, but don't confuse them with hybrid teas. Tea roses gained popularity in the latter part of the 19th century, and many are still with us today. Hybrid teas are a totally different class of roses and didn't start to gain popularity until after World War II. Today's hybrid teas got their part of their pointed bloom shape from the tea roses.

While they are only hardy to Zone 7 or the milder parts of Zone 6, tea roses make excellent garden roses. They bloom almost continually during the season, come in a broad range of colors, have a pleasing upright growth habit, and often bear some fragrance. Size can range from 4 to 6 to even 8 feet if left unchecked. Luckily, they take very well to being trimmed and shaped all season.

Their disease resistance is excellent—particularly in the southeastern United States. In fact, many rose experts consider them to be among the best roses for gardening in that part of the country. For instructions on how to prune them, see "Pruning Roses That Build a Structure" on p. 88.

VARIETY: 'Clementina Carbonieri'
ICRAR Code: None
Bloom Color: Salmon pink
Zones: 7–9
Height: 3–5 feet
Width: 3–5 feet

Fragrance: Strong fragrance
Flowering: Flowers from spring to fall
Growth Habit: Bushy, upright growth
Foliage: Medium green
Bloom Type: Fully double
Light Conditions: Full sun

'Clementina Carbonieri'

VARIETY: 'Mons. Tiller'
ICRAR Code: None
Bloom Color: Apricot pink
Zones: 7–9
Height: 4–6 feet
Width: 3–4 feet
Fragrance: Moderate fragrance
Flowering: Flowers from spring to fall
Growth Habit: Bushy, upright growth
Foliage: Medium green
Bloom Type: Fully double
Light Conditions: Full sun

'Mons. Tiller'

VARIETY: 'Mme. Berkley'
ICRAR Code: None
Bloom Color: Apricot pink
Zones: 7–9
Height: 3–5 feet
Width: 3–4 feet
Fragrance: Strong fragrance
Flowering: Flowers from spring to fall
Growth Habit: Bushy, upright growth

Foliage: Medium green
Bloom Type: Fully double
Light Conditions: Full sun

VARIETY: 'William R. Smith'
ICRAR Code: None
Bloom Color: Yellow/pink
Zones: 7–9
Height: 4–6 feet
Width: 3–4 feet
Fragrance: Strong fragrance
Flowering: Flowers from spring to fall
Growth Habit: Bushy, upright growth
Foliage: Medium green
Bloom Type: Fully double
Light Conditions: Full sun

VARIETY: 'Souv. d'un Ami
ICRAR Code: None
Bloom Color: Medium pink
Zones: 7–9
Height: 4–6 feet
Width: 3–4 feet
Fragrance: Strong fragrance
Flowering: Flowers from spring to fall
Growth Habit: Bushy, upright growth
Foliage: Purple on young leaves maturing to dark green
Bloom Type: Fully double
Light Conditions: Full sun

'Souv. d'un Ami'

Earth-Kind® Roses

LANDSCAPE USES:
- Borders (excluding climbers)
- Containers (shorter shrubs)
- Ground covers
- Mass planting (excluding climbers)
- Masses of roses (excluding climbers)
- Climbing roses

- Rose as hedges (taller shrubs)
- Roses as screens (the climbers)
- Roses over rock walls (the ground covers)
- Creative rose growing

Earth-Kind roses are a group of roses that have passed a very grueling three-year trial. After planting, the only thing they receive is mulch. Water is supplied only for the first year to get them established. After that, the only water they get is what nature provides. They are never sprayed or fertilized with anything—even organics.

The initial group of Earth-Kind roses was tested in Texas under the guidance of Dr. Steven George at Texas A&M University. There are now test gardens in other parts of the country.

Their growth habits vary widely, so evaluate each one individually for garden use. Some of the taller shrubs can be grown as short climbers in warmer climates. Basic garden rose care brings out the best in them.

VARIETY: 'Mutabalis'
ICRAR Code: None
Bloom Color: Yellow, orange, pink, and crimson
Zones: 7–11
Height: 6–8 feet
Width: 4–6 feet
Fragrance: None
Flowering: Flowers from spring to fall
Growth Habit: Bushy, upright growth
Foliage: Dark green
Bloom Type: Single
Light Conditions: Full sun, can take dappled light

VARIETY: 'Belinda's Dream'
ICRAR Code: None
Bloom Color: Medium pink
Zones: 5–9
Height: 4–6 feet
Width: 3–4 feet
Fragrance: Moderate fragrance
Flowering: Flowers from spring to fall

Growth Habit: Bushy, upright growth
Foliage: Medium green
Bloom Type: Fully double
Light Conditions: Full sun

'Belinda's Dream'

VARIETY: 'New Dawn'
Normally grown as a climber, here 'New Dawn' is grown as a standard or tree rose.
ICRAR Code: None
Bloom Color: Blush pink
Zones: 4–10
Height: 15–20 feet
Width: N/A
Fragrance: Slight fragrance
Flowering: Flowers from spring to fall
Growth Habit: Climbing rose
Foliage: Dark green
Bloom Type: Fully double
Light Conditions: Full sun

'New Dawn'

VARIETY: 'La Marne'
ICRAR Code: None
Bloom Color: Pink with white center
Zones: 4–9
Height: 4–5 feet
Width: 4–5 feet
Fragrance: Slight fragrance
Flowering: Flowers from spring to fall
Growth Habit: Bushy, upright growth

Foliage: Medium green
Bloom Type: Semi-double
Light Conditions: Full sun

VARIETY: 'Reve d'Or'
ICRAR Code: None
Bloom Color: Apricot
Zones: 7–9
Height: 12–15 feet
Width: N/A
Fragrance: Moderate fragrance
Flowering: Flowers from spring to fall
Growth Habit: Climbing rose
Foliage: Purple on young leaves maturing to dark green
Bloom Type: Double
Light Conditions: Full sun

'Reve d'Or'

Kordes Family of Roses from Wilhelm Kordes & Sonne

LANDSCAPE USES:
- Borders (excluding climbers)
- Containers (shorter varieties)
- Ground covers (only ground-cover varieties)
- Mass planting (excluding climbers)
- Masses of roses (excluding climbers)
- Climbing roses (only the climbers)
- Hedges (taller varieties)
- Climbing rose screens
- Roses over rock walls (ground-cover varieties)
- Creative rose growing

The German firm of Kordes (breeder code KOR) has been breeding roses for well over 100 years. They were one of the first nurseries to stop spraying their test fields and consequently have made great strides in the disease resistance of their roses.

The growth habits of their work vary from ground cover to small shrubs to large shrubs to climbers, so evaluate each one individually for garden use. They have a wide range of colors and bloom shapes, so there is much to choose from.

VARIETY: Flamingo Kolorscape™
ICRAR Code: 'KORhopiko'
Bloom Color: Hot pink
Zones: 4–10
Height: 3–4 feet
Width: 2–3 feet
Fragrance: Light fruity scent
Flowering: Flowers from spring to fall
Growth Habit: Compact form slightly taller than wide
Foliage: Purple on young leaves maturing to medium green
Bloom Type: Semi-double
Light Conditions: Full sun to light shade

Flamingo Kolorscape

VARIETY: Solero Vigorosa®
ICRAR Code: 'KORsupigel'
Bloom Color: Yellow
Zones: 5–10
Height: 2–3 feet
Width: 3 feet
Fragrance: Light tea rose scent
Flowering: Flowers from spring to fall
Growth Habit: Low mounding bushy
Foliage: Medium green
Bloom Type: Fully double
Light Conditions: Full sun to light shade

VARIETY: Brothers Grimm™
ICRAR Code: 'KORassenet'
Bloom Color: Yellow with red edges
Zones: 5–10
Height: 4 feet
Width: 3 feet
Fragrance: Light fruity fragrance
Flowering: Flowers from spring to fall
Growth Habit: Bushy, upright growth
Foliage: Purple on young leaves maturing to dark green
Bloom Type: Double
Light Conditions: Full sun to light shade

VARIETY: Mandarin Ice™
ICRAR Code: 'KORplumbo'
Bloom Color: Orange red with white reverse
Zones: 5–10
Height: 3–4 feet
Width: 3 feet
Fragrance: None
Flowering: Flowers from spring to fall
Growth Habit: Bushy, mounding growth
Foliage: Medium green
Bloom Type: Double
Light Conditions: Full sun to light shade

Mandarin Ice

VARIETY: Black Forest™
ICRAR Code: 'KORschwill'
Bloom Color: Red
Zones: 4–10
Height: 3–4 feet
Width: 3 feet
Fragrance: None
Flowering: Flowers from spring to fall
Growth Habit: Compact, mounding, bushy growth
Foliage: Dark green
Bloom Type: Semi-double
Light Conditions: Full sun to light shade

VARIETY: Kordes Golden Gate™
ICRAR Code: 'KORgolgat'
Bloom Color: Yellow
Zones: 5–10
Height: 8–14 feet
Width: 3 feet
Fragrance: Strong spicy and citrus scent
Flowering: Flowers from spring to fall
Growth Habit: Climbing rose
Foliage: Dark green
Bloom Type: Double
Light Conditions: Full sun to light shade

Golden Gate

VARIETY: Roxy™
ICRAR Code: 'KORsineo'
Bloom Color: Lavender pink
Zones: 4–10
Height: 1–1½ feet
Width: 2–2½ feet
Fragrance: Light, sweet scent
Flowering: Flowers from spring to fall
Growth Habit: Ground cover, bushy growth
Foliage: Purple on young leaves maturing to medium green
Bloom Type: Fully double
Light Conditions: Full sun to light shade

David Austin
Family of Roses
from David
Austin

LANDSCAPE USES:
- Borders (excluding climbers)
- Containers (shorter varieties)
- Mass planting (excluding climbers)
- Masses of roses (excluding climbers)

- **Climbing roses (climbers and larger shrubs in warm climates)**

We owe the idea of roses with an old-fashioned look coupled with modern repeat flowering characteristics to David Austin (breeder code AUS), as he is the person who started it all. From a breeding program that is more than five decades old have come forth some lovely garden roses.

In recent years, breeders have been focusing more on disease resistance, replacing many older varieties with ones they feel are better performers healthwise. (That being said, there are some gems among those older David Austin rose varieties.)

Their growth habit is mostly all shrub shaped, with sizes from 2 feet to 6 feet or more. Many of the larger shrubs can be grown as short climbers in warmer climates and are well suited for pillars and low fences. There a few true climbers among the collection.

Some of the taller shrubs respond well to being cutting back hard after each bloom flush (meaning to half their mature height). This will produce better subsequent flushes. Because of their diversity of growth habit, evaluate each variety individually for garden use. Almost of all of them will flower well with only four to five hours of morning sun.

VARIETY: 'Munstead Wood'
ICRAR Code: 'AUSbernard'
Bloom Color: Deep crimson
Zones: 5–9
Height: 3–4 feet
Width: 2–2½ feet
Fragrance: Old rose fragrance
Flowering: Flowers from spring to fall
Growth Habit: Bushy, rounded growth

Foliage: Bronze on young leaves maturing to medium green
Bloom Type: Fully double
Light Conditions: Full sun

'Munstead Wood'

VARIETY: 'Carding Mill'
ICRAR Code: 'AUSwest'
Bloom Color: Pink, apricot, and yellow
Zones: 5–9
Height: 4–5 feet
Width: 3–4 feet
Fragrance: Strong myrrh fragrance
Flowering: Flowers from spring to fall
Growth Habit: Bushy, rounded growth habit
Foliage: Medium green
Bloom Type: Fully double
Light Conditions: Full sun

VARIETY: 'The Generous Gardener'
ICRAR Code: 'AUSdrawn'
Bloom Color: Soft pink
Zones: 5–9
Height: 5–8 feet
Width: 4 feet
Fragrance: Strong old rose fragrance
Flowering: Flowers from spring to fall
Growth Habit: Bushy, spreading growth; also short climber in warm climates
Foliage: Medium green
Bloom Type: Fully double
Light Conditions: Full sun

VARIETY: 'Molineux'
ICRAR Code: 'AUSmol'
Bloom Color: Rich yellow
Zones: 5–9
Height: 3–4 feet
Width: 2–3 feet
Fragrance: Tea rose fragrance
Flowering: Flowers from spring to fall
Growth Habit: Bushy, upright growth

Foliage: Medium green
Bloom Type: Fully double
Light Conditions: Full sun

'Molineux'

VARIETY: 'The Alnwick Rose'
ICRAR Code: 'AUSgrab'
Bloom Color: Rich pink
Zones: 5–9
Height: 4–5 feet
Width: 2–3 feet
Fragrance: Old rose fragrance
Flowering: Flowers from spring to fall
Growth Habit: Bushy, upright growth
Foliage: Medium green
Bloom Type: Fully double
Light Conditions: Full sun

VARIETY: 'Princess Alexandra of Kent'
ICRAR Code: 'AUSmerchant'
Bloom Color: Warm pink
Zones: 5–9
Height: 3–4 feet
Width: 2–3 feet
Fragrance: Tea rose fragrance
Flowering: Flowers from spring to fall
Growth Habit: Bushy, rounded growth
Foliage: Medium green
Bloom Type: Fully double
Light Conditions: Full sun

'Princess Alexandra of Kent'

Appendix

A Brief History of Roses

Rose growing wasn't always so complicated. In fact, for thousands of years, it involved no work at all. Mother Nature herself created the first roses, which are species roses. By estimate, more than 100 species of roses exist. The arguments as to what defines a species rose are numerous, and this is not the place for that. Suffice it to say that species roses have been on this earth long before man, long before cultivated gardens, and long before anyone knew what an outward-facing bud eye was.

These species roses survived without any care and still do today. Many a hedgerow in England, a mountainside in China, or an old homestead in America still contain these original roses thriving happily under the hand of Mother Nature. And fortunately, many gardeners still grow and enjoy them in their own gardens.

Over time and with a little help from the birds and the bees, pollen from the species roses was mixed and other forms of cultivated or "hybrid" roses began to emerge. Some of the earliest known to the Western world are what are known as the "Old European roses." Groups like gallicas, damasks, centifolias, albas, Portlands, and mosses poured forth perfume mostly during the spring bloom season. In Asia, the China roses and tea roses began to emerge, carrying with them repeat flowering qualities rarely seen in the Western world and destined to remain hidden from Western view until the times of the clipper ships.

Like their native ancestors, these roses too thrived on benign neglect. The weaker varieties among them were weeded out by either the hand of nature or the hoe of the gardener, and the stronger ones persisted by being passed from garden to garden via cuttings or shoots that emerged next to the parent plant in the warmth of springtime.

Many a rose made its way across America in a Conestoga wagon tucked somewhere between the family clock and the frying pan used to make "Hoppin' John." Upon arrival at the new homestead, it was planted, watered, and left to grow under the same conditions those early settlers encountered. Over time, their true names were forgotten, and they became known simply as "Grandma's Red Rose" or "Aunt Sally's Pink Climber." Many survive today as "found roses" that are rustled by dedicated rosarians. Names like 'Charleston Graveyard', 'Angles Camp White Tea', and 'Natchitoches Noisette' are as much a testament to the conditions they thrived under as they are to the locations where they were rediscovered.

In Europe, roses found their way into almost every garden. Some were grown for their beauty, and some were grown for medicinal purposes. *Rosa gallica officinalis* became better known as 'Apothecary's Rose' for that very reason. The ability to retain its perfume in the dried petals was just another reason to tuck it amid the hollyhocks in the garden.

Rose hips became valued as a rich source of vitamin C and were carried by sailors on long voyages to prevent scurvy. As recently as World War II, rose hips were grown in victory gardens to replace the vitamin C normally found in citrus fruits, which at the time were unavailable in cooler climates. I would wager a bet that the roses producing those hips were treated just like all the other plants in those hundreds of thousands of victory gardens grown during wartime. Imagine if those "victory roses" needed complicated spraying and feeding programs. I suspect they would have been used more as compost than a source for vitamin C.

THE BIRTH OF ROSE BREEDING

During the 1800s, repeat flowering roses from China began to arrive on the sails of the clipper ships. Four of them, 'Slater's Crimson China', 'Parson's Pink China', 'Hume's Blush Tea-Scented China', and 'Park's Yellow Tea-Scented China' became collectively known as the Four Stud Chinas. In time, they were crossed with the Old European roses. Like any cross of a repeat flowering rose with a spring flowering rose, their first offspring did not repeat. But subsequent generations did. From these the Bourbon roses developed, as did Noisettes. China and tea roses also continued to develop. All are roses that are relatively easy to care for and are grown widely throughout the world.

During this era, an English cattle breeder named Henry Bennett introduced the record keeping and purposeful crossing of cattle to achieve desired qualities into rose breeding. Until then, rose breeding was mostly left to whims of nature as hips were harvested, seedlings grown, and roses released into commerce without much knowledge of parentage and without intent of achieving certain qualities.

Henry Bennett purposefully took pollen from one rose to another, noted the cross, and documented the results. He discovered over time that he could influence the outcome of the roses he was breeding by using certain roses again and again. The result is rose breeding much as it's done today. The fact that today's talented breeders can breed for characteristics such as disease resistance, stripes, and shorter growth habit can be traced back to Mr. Bennett.

As roses continued to be crossed, there emerged a class of roses known as hybrid perpetuals. They are a result of taking the first-generation spring-flowering offspring of the Old European roses crossed with China roses, and then crossing them with the Portland roses (also known as damask perpetuals). The intent was to get the hardiness of the damask perpetuals to combine with the ranges of color

and the constant flowering qualities found in the Chinas. What typically emerged were roses with huge cabbage-like blossoms perched atop what were then long stems.

As with anything new, these became the rage, and within a short time there were thousands of hybrid perpetuals in commerce. They were also developed simultaneously with the rise of the popularity of rose shows. In 1876, the Rev. Dean Hole began the Royal National Rose Society in England and promoted rose shows as a way of drawing in new members and educating the public about roses. As the popularity of roses shows increased, so did the intensity of the competition. The breeding of hybrid perpetuals became refined to achieve roses whose value lay more in their ability to produce great cut flowers for exhibition than to be a great garden plant. Length of time the cut flower was held on the stem and form were valued over ease of growth and disease resistance. Endless hours were spent fussing over them to get that Queen of Show, and the public began to believe if their roses at home didn't look like the ones on the winner's table, they had somehow failed as rose gardeners. Does that sound familiar?

The Victorian era was a time of great wealth, with large greenhouses on country estates and huge staffs of gardeners both in the United States and abroad. This meant time and money were of no object in the pursuit of "perfection." Roses were now also becoming grown solely for the beauty of the flower. This meant some rose growers grew roses for their garden value and some for their cut flower/exhibition value. Both were hardworking, dedicated groups, but the result was that two different types of roses began to emerge: one for cut flower/exhibition and the other for garden roses.

The introduction of the first hybrid tea in the late 1800s was by most markers an improvement upon the hybrid perpetuals, a class becoming known for being difficult and finicky to grow—this should also sound familiar! The same Henry Bennett is considered by many to be the father of the hybrid tea and achieved his success by deliberately crossing hybrid perpetuals with tea roses. From the hybrid perpetuals, he took the long stems and the large blooms appearing solely on the stem. From the teas, he took their continual flowering and long petals, which gradually became the high-centered hybrid tea bloom of today.

THE EVOLUTION OF ROSES

Many rose historians consider there to be three distinct eras of hybrid teas, and they are separated by the two World Wars of the 20th century. Those bred before the war were still closely related to their tea cousins in that the shrubs were rounded and their stems still did not quite achieve the length of today's hybrid teas. Between the wars, roses saw great progress in both form and stem length. At the end of World War II, one of the most popular hybrid teas of all time was released: the 'Peace' rose. 'Peace' was arguably one of the first roses to truly look like today's hybrid tea roses. Long stems, high pointed centers, and single flowers per stem set the benchmark for hybrid teas to come.

All this activity did not mean garden roses were being neglected. Many hybrid teas, and particularly the early ones, made excellent garden roses. In addition, three of the finest garden rose classes we have now were introduced during this era. The hybrid musks were developed by the Rev. Joseph Pemberton in England during the early 20th century. The polyantha came into being in the late 1880s and continued to flourish for some time. Floribunda roses were born and began to fully realize their potential under the visionary eye of the rose breeder Gene Boerner, also known as "Papa Floribunda." Many great

garden roses from these classes are still with us today.

Rose growing, while still popular in the early part of the 20th century, was no longer set against the backdrop of the leisure time of the Victorian era. Two wars, a great depression, and people moving to the cities meant attention was elsewhere. However, after World War II, the United States in particular entered an era of unprecedented prosperity. The Marshall Plan in Europe meant they too would join in, although it would take longer. In addition, chemicals were suddenly cheap, popular, and naively considered safe to use. The vision of *Leave It to Beaver's* June Cleaver tending roses in her skirt, pearls, and coiffed hair had arrived.

Hybrid teas were the rage and, as mentioned, the form of 'Peace' rose set the standard to be built upon. Cheap chemicals meant disease resistance was not an issue. Many families had only one working parent, the soccer mom had yet to arrive on the scene, and homes in the suburbs meant space for gardening. The demand was for high-centered hybrid teas on long stems, and the rose industry complied. Fragrance began to lose importance, as did disease resistance and vigor. Why worry about it when you could hop down to your local hardware store and buy DDT? Many roses that were really meant for the cut flower/exhibition market were now being sold as garden roses, which for the most part they were not.

Still, some rose breeding firms kept the two separate. They bred roses for the cut flower industry and a totally separate line of roses as garden roses. The German firm of Kordes Roses International is a prime example, as is the French firm Delbard. And some, like Peter Beales Roses in the United Kingdom, simply bred only garden roses. But these garden roses were mostly confined to Europe, where the line between them and cut flower/exhibition varieties was kept fairly distinct. In addition, Europe and most of the rest of the world has always had an aversion to chemicals for the home market.

BACK TO BASICS

In the latter part of the 20th century, as the United States became more environmentally aware, a few chemicals were taken off the market. While many fine hybrid teas were able to thrive without them, many a diva rose, which up to now could only be grown with chemicals, began to flounder. Since those roses had been marketed and sold at the expense of the true garden roses, it meant many home gardeners were suddenly faced with a plant that was difficult to grow, wouldn't flourish, and in many instances died off within a few years. Roses began to get the reputation as being fussy, weak, and needing a great deal of care. Suddenly the image of June Cleaver gardening in her pearls turned into the reality of our mothers slaving over their roses, and we didn't want to have to work that hard.

That gardeners were beginning to look for easier-to-grow roses is evidenced in the resurgent interest in the old garden roses during this time. Old garden roses had a reputation for being disease resistant and easy to grow. It's a reputation they had earned, because over time the poor ones had disappeared and the stronger ones survived. I would suspect in 100 years, the hybrid tea class will have gone through the same culling process, and someone reading this book will wonder what the fuss was all about!

In the 1990s, the David Austin roses took flight in this country. They not only had an old-fashioned look and could be planted among other plants, but they also had fragrance. They were marketed as garden roses, and once again the line between garden roses and cut flower/exhibition roses began to strongly emerge—particularly in the United States.

The first part of this century has seen a rapid decline in sales of hybrid tea roses. This is not necessarily because they are bad roses (a lot of newer hybrid teas make terrific garden roses), but because the decades before had built the perception they were fussy, were disease prone, bore little fragrance, and had little use in the garden.

Sales of shrub roses began to rise, beginning with the release of the Knock Out rose in 2000. Bred by William Radler, The Knock Out Family of Roses began to bring us back to garden roses. They make terrific low-care shrubs, and their skyrocketing sales reemphasize that the desire for disease-resistant, easy-to-grow garden roses is back. Today's breeders are meeting that demand, and roses from Europe and beyond are also becoming more readily available in the United States. Roses are coming full circle by going back to what they were for the vast majority of their history: a great flowering shrub for the garden. A garden rose.

Should a Rose's Growth Habit Determine Its Class?

Let's begin with the simple question: How does a rose get its classification? When a new rose is hybridized, someone registers it with the International Cultivar Registration Authority for Roses (ICRAR). The person who registers the rose is usually the breeder, but sometimes it can be the nursery of introduction acting on the breeder's behalf. It is that person who determines what class (hybrid tea, alba, hybrid musk, floribunda, and so on) the rose will fall into.

How does that person determine the rose's class? Most often by its parentage: If a rose is the result of a cross from two China roses, then the rose is classed as a China. Sometimes it might be by growth habit: Many roses have such complicated parentage in their backgrounds, they don't always come "true" to their parentage. It's kind of like the redhead in a family of brunettes. And sometimes if the registrar isn't sure, the nursery or breeder may, for commercial reasons, register it in a class that is currently selling well. Many a rose ended up as a hybrid tea that way, and many roses today are being put into the shrub category because hybrid teas aren't selling.

By now, you get the point that there isn't really a formally structured way of doing this. Unlike the standard nomenclature established by Linnaeus, who looked for order in the plant kingdom, the current method of rose classification is a loose system that does not serve the rose community or roses well, in my opinion.

I feel the rose classification system, while important for the work of botanists, is also important for the rose lover. Rose lovers would like a simple system whereby the rose's class gives them an idea of how the rose will grow in their garden. If a rose is classed as a hybrid wichurana, it should have lax rambling canes. A gallica should flower in spring and be upright. A Portland shouldn't get overly tall, and a shrub should be just that—a shrub. To me, the first criteria for classing a rose should be growth habit regardless of parentage.

There is historical evidence for this argument, and it comes right from the ICRAR. Let's look at the history of 'La France', the rose many consider to be the first hybrid tea. Most evidence points to it being a seedling of 'Mme. Falcot'—a tea rose. So why not classify it as a tea? Well, simply because it was something new and therefore a new class was introduced—the hybrid tea. Other classes, such as floribunda, polyantha, and the newer class mini-flora, were all created to accommodate roses that simply did not belong to any other group because of their growth habit—be it flower, size, or both. This system works fine as long as it's consistent. Sadly, it no longer is, and the old roses in particular have been the victims.

COMBINING CLASSES

In 1993, the ICRAR recognized approximately 31 classes pertaining to old roses, and by 2000 it was down to 22. So what's missing, and do they really matter? Many think they do. For example, China and hybrid China and Bourbon and hybrid Bourbon were, until recently, separate classes. Then they were merged into hybrid China and hybrid Bourbon, respectively. Some argued they were all hybrids, because they were all crossed with other roses. But they are not at all similar if you examine how they perform in the garden.

Hybrid Chinas and hybrid Bourbons are the result of crosses between Chinas or Bourbons with spring-flowering European roses. The results are roses that, while they might have a longer spring flush than a gallica, do not for the most part repeat-flower. That is a very different rose from a China, which during the season is constantly in flower, or repeat-flowering Bourbons, which at minimum

also bring forth a wonderful fall bloom as well as spring. In addition, many hybrid Chinas are tall growers—again, completely different from the smaller Chinas.

So under the current system, 'Coup de Hebe', a Bourbon that flowers in spring, is in the same class as 'Louise Odier', a Bourbon rarely without flowers. 'Brennus', a China that for me grows 7 feet high and does not repeat, is in the same class as 'Comtesse du Cayla', which flowers all season and stays around 3 feet.

Add to this confusion the Noisette class, which is a complete mess. The Noisettes at their birth in Charleston, South Carolina, were shrublike in habit and bloomed mostly in shades of white and pink. Then they were crossed with climbing tea roses, and the result is a group of roses that are distinctly climbers and come in shades of white to yellow to apricot. They are very different from the first Noisettes, and the "nickname" given them is "tea-Noisette." Many feel they are a distinctly different class and should be separated as such, but up to now they all remain Noisettes. Not much comfort to the person who buys the Noisette 'Mary Washington' to cover her arbor and finds it only grows 4 feet high.

So where do these roses go when their class is no longer officially used? Some, like the aforementioned Bourbon and China groups, are simply merged. However, some are simply lumped into the shrub class, and because of this, the shrub class is one that doesn't mean anything anymore. The most extreme example of this is the rose 'Montecito', which for many years was a hybrid gigantea until that class was dropped and it was dumped in the shrub class. The problem is 'Montecito' grows up trees and easily reaches 50 feet in height. Hardly a shrub! Luckily, cooler heads have prevailed, and 'Montecito' once again rests among the hybrid giganteas.

The good news is there is an attempt under way to sort this out. The ICRAR Classification Committee is working through the roses and attempting to come up with a cohesive system. The balancing act faced by this hardworking group is to avoid ending up with so many different classes as to be unwieldy, but to have enough classes to bring order to the system. This will take time, as there are as many opinions as there are roses. But if they use growth habit as their primary guide, a logical system will emerge. After all, it seems the roses themselves should have the final say.

Rose Classes

Another useful way to begin searching out other garden roses is by using the rose classes as a guide. As with most things, it's not a perfect system, but it's a good place to start. As always, before you make that final purchase, check with other local rose growers and on the forums. I asked Richard Beales, of Peter Beales Roses U.K., to help come up with a list of classes that make good garden roses both here and in the United Kingdom. Some of these are modern and some as old as time itself.

ALBAS

A very healthy group of roses that can be used as climbers or shrubs. All are fragrant and, although spring flowering only, are very charismatic in that their gray-green foliage make perfect backdrops for summer and fall flowering perennials and roses. In terms of size, they can get tall—up to 6 feet. They are very hardy, with some withstanding Zone 4, and available mostly by mail order.

ALBA ROSE STANDOUTS
1. 'Mme. Plantier'
2. 'Maiden's Blush'
3. 'Mme. Legras de Saint Germain'
4. 'Félicité Parmentier'
5. 'Königin von Dänemark'

CHINA

This group of roses is invaluable in that the roses stay on the short side—something important in today's smaller gardens. In addition, they are usually healthy, flower continuously in summer, and have an important genealogy as ancestors to modern roses. Many do well in pots, and they excel in mass plantings. In the United States, they are hardy to Zone 7 and even Zone 6, if they are sheltered from the wind. They are mostly available by mail order.

CHINA ROSE STANDOUTS
1. 'Papa Hemeray'
2. 'Spice'
3. 'Pink Pet'
4. 'Old Blush'
5. 'Cramoiso Superieur'

ENGLISH

This lovely group of roses was "invented" by David Austin by crossing old roses with modern shrubs. The goal was to combine the look, feel, and fragrance of the old roses with the reblooming and disease-resistance qualities of modern roses. While originally associated with Mr. Austin, today this group has come to include many from other rose breeders as long as they have that old-fashioned look. Mostly all hardy to Zone 5, they come in many different sizes and shapes. They are widely available in garden centers and by mail order.

ENGLISH ROSE STANDOUTS
1. 'Munstead Wood'
2. 'Carding Mill'
3. 'Molineux'
4. 'Princess Alexandria of Kent'
5. The Alnwick Rose

FLORIBUNDA

These roses have been developed over the last 100 years or so, and some of them make superb garden plants, especially if grown in groups. They are usually healthier than hybrid teas, and a few of the older varieties of quieter colors fit comfortably among the older roses of all types. Their smaller size—on average 3 to 5 feet tall—makes them welcome additions to the garden. Many are hardy to Zone 5. They are widely available in garden centers and by mail order.

FLORIBUNDA STANDOUTS
1. 'Sexy Rexy'
2. 'Gruss An Aachen'
3. 'Margaret Merrill'
4. 'Iceberg'
5. 'Scentimental'

GALLICAS

They are spring flowering, but make up for this by having some of the most beautiful and fragrant flowers of the old garden roses. Grown as shrubs, they are usually easy to accommodate in any situation. Fans of purple colors will love the gallicas; the shade runs rampant through the class. They are hardy to Zone 4 and some even beyond. They need a winter chill to bloom well, so I would advise against growing them above a Zone 7 (and even that might be pushing it). They are available mostly by mail order.

GALLICA STANDOUTS
1. 'Charles de Mills'
2. 'Cardinal de Richelieu'
3. 'Rosa Mundi'
4. 'Tuscany Superb'
5. 'Complicata'

GROUND COVER

This is a recently emerging class of roses that are very useful. The first introductions to this group had a growth habit that was more of a low arching shrub, but newer varieties have a true spreading growth habit. Just don't confuse them with ground cover that you can walk on! Many are hardy down to Zone 4. They are widely available in garden centers and by mail order.

1. **Apricot Drift**
2. **Oso Easy Paprika**
3. **'Ruby Ruby'**
4. **Pink Drift**
5. **'Roxy'**

HYBRID MUSKS

A class created by the Rev. Joseph Pemberton in England, this is a superb group of remontant (repeat flowering) shrub roses, almost all of which were developed between the two World Wars. They are easy to maintain and keep healthy. Some are quite capable of making small, continuous flowering climbers if grown on walls or given support. They can handle temperatures as cold as Zone 5 and also seem to thrive in heat. A handful are available in garden centers, and the rest can be purchased by mail order.

1. **'Wilhelm'**
2. **'Darlow's Enigma'**
3. **'Buff Beauty'**
4. **'Prosperity'**
5. **'Daybreak'**

MINI-FLORA

Over the last 20 years, a class of roses began to emerge that in growth and flower size seemed halfway between miniature roses and floribunda roses. They were christened "mini-flora" and are becoming widely available. Perfect for today's smaller gardens, they are close to the flower size of the larger roses with the growth size and habit of smaller, miniature roses. They are easy to care for, and some are hardy even to Zone 4. They are widely available in garden centers and by mail order.

1. **'Bordure Nacree'**
2. **Smart & Sassy**
3. **'Music Box'**
4. **Oso Easy Cherry Pie**
5. **'Jean Giono'**

MODERN SHRUBS

These are a group of roses that have been developed since the end of World War II. They are of mixed progeny, almost all are continuously flowering, and they are good in areas where space permits them to develop their own personality. A handful can be grown as small climbers if placed against some form of support. With this group, it is especially important to judge each variety individually and speak with other rose growers in your area about the ones you are thinking of growing. Almost all will be hardy to Zone 6, with many hardy to Zone 5, and some even to Zone 4 or lower. Size can vary from 3 feet to 8 feet or more. They are widely available in garden centers and by mail order.

1. **The Knock Out Rose**
2. **'Dames De Chenonceau'**
3. **'Flamenco'**
4. **Carefree Delight**
5. **'Abbaye de Cluny'**

NOISETTES

Created in Charleston, South Carolina, by a rice planter named John Champney, these roses are a class of mostly repeat-blooming climbers with colors ranging from white through yellows and reds. Almost without exception, they are fragrant with good, healthy foliage. Some of the earlier Noisettes like 'Mary Washington' are shrubs, so do some homework. It was when they were crossed with teas that they almost all became climbers. They are hardy to Zone 6, and some are grown in Zone 5 in sheltered spots or with winter protection. A handful are available in garden centers, and the rest can be purchased through mail order.

1. **'Reve d'Or'**
2. **'Blush Noisette'**
3. **'Mme. Alfred Carriere'**
4. **'Alister Stella Gray'**
5. **'Crepescule'**

POLYANTHAS

These are a very underused and underappreciated group of first-class garden roses. The smaller blooms appear in clusters all season long on shrubs packed with proportionately sized foliage. Most stay under 3 feet and will spread as wide or more. They are very healthy and easily hardy to Zone 5. A handful can be found in garden centers and the rest are available by mail order.

1. **'The Fairy'**
2. **'Margo Koster'**
3. **'Marie Pavie'**
4. **'Perle d'Or'**
5. **Marjorie Fair**

PORTLANDS

Our northern gardening friends rightly lament that it is difficult to find hardy, repeat-flowering shrubs. Look no further, because all Portlands flower continuously through the summer, and most have a built-in resistance to diseases. They are, without exception, fragrant and easy to grow, especially in group planting or bedding. They are easily hardy to Zone 5 and some to Zone 4. Their average height is 3 to 5 feet, which is ideal for any garden. They are available mostly by mail order.

RAMBLERS

Almost all the ramblers of both wichurana and multiflora origin have the "wow" factor when in full bloom. Within their ranks is a complete spectrum of color. They are healthy and, if necessary, will tolerate impoverished soil and harsher weather conditions. An excellent use of these ramblers is as a backdrop to repeat flowering climbers. In spring, all the roses are in bloom, and for the rest of the season, the healthy and abundant foliage of the ramblers accents the repeat flowering roses. They are easily hardy to cold climates of Zone 4 or lower. They are mostly available by mail order.

RUGOSAS

These are the roses that grow wild in the sandy soil on the beaches in places like Maine. These must be classified as the healthiest of all roses. Almost all are fragrant and repeat their flowers in succession throughout the summer. They have durable dark green foliage and most of the single-flowered varieties pro-duce an excellent crop of bright red hips every autumn. All make superb hedging plants. They are easily hardy to Zone 4 and Zone 3. One thing to keep in mind is that they hate spraying of any kind on their leaves. I have also found in hotter climates it is best to plant them in a location so that by mid-day they are out of the scorching sun, as it will burn their leaves. Some are widely available in garden centers and the rest can be purchased by mail order.

SPECIES

Among the species roses are many that make superb garden plants. Although few are remontant, they are invariably healthy, and most produce a superb crop of brightly colored hips. Hardiness will vary, so again, check with rose growers in your area or on the Internet forums. Sizes vary widely, so do a little home-work, because when they get big, they get very big. They are mostly available by mail order.

TEA

These are often confused with hybrid tea roses, but they are totally different. Tea roses gained popular-ity in the late 19th century and were bred to be outstanding garden roses. Remember, at that time modern garden chemicals did not exist. Hybrid teas, as we've previously discussed, were bred more for their long stems in a time when chemi-cals were readily available to treat disease.

Tea roses continually bear their blooms all season long and come in most every color found in the rose world—including bicolor. Their open growth habit and rounded shape are very pleasing in any garden setting. In warm climates, some can grow to 7 feet or more, but generally they stay in the 5-foot range. They also don't mind being regularly trimmed. They are hardy to Zone 7 and can handle Zone 6 if sheltered from freezing winds. They are mostly available by mail order.

Rose Classes by Landscape Use

LANDSCAPE USE SUGGESTED CLASS: Use with information on Rose Classes pp. 171–173.

GROUND COVER	Ground cover Some ramblers	
SHORT BUSH	China Polyantha Some shrub Some floribunda Floribunda Mini-flora	
MEDIUM BUSH	Some floribunda Tea Some English Portland Some shrub	Gallica Hybrid musk Rugosa
TALL BUSH	Some shrub Some species Albas	
HEDGE	Floribunda Tea Species Some shrub	Albas Hybrid musk Rugosa
POTS	China Some shrub Polyantha Floribundas Mini-flora	
PILLARING	Noisette Some English Some shrub Some albas Some hybrid musks	
TERRACES	Ground cover for the front row Polyantha, mini-flora, and small shrub for a back row	

Metric Equivalency Chart

US MEASUREMENT	METRIC
½ inch	1.27 Centimeters
1 inch	2.54 Centimeters
1 foot	30.48 Centimeters
1 yard (also 3 feet)	0.91 Meter
1 teaspoon (tsp.)	4.92 Milliliters
1 tablespoon (Tbs.)	14.78 Milliliters
1 pint	0.47 Liter
1 quart	0.94 Liter
1 gallon	3.78 Liters

Zone Map

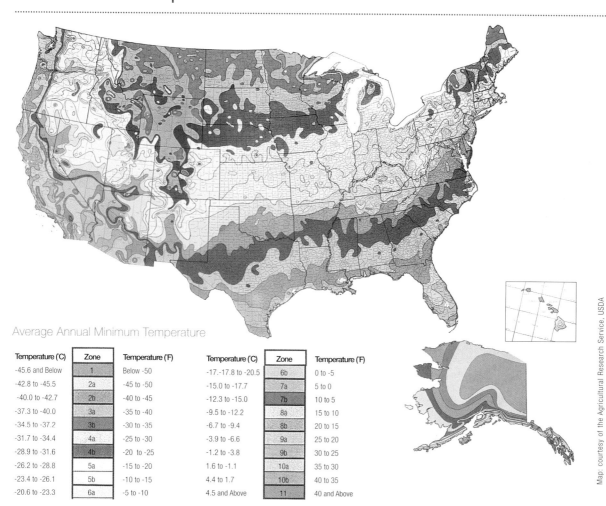

Average Annual Minimum Temperature

Temperature (C)	Zone	Temperature (F)	Temperature (C)	Zone	Temperature (F)
-45.6 and Below	1	Below -50	-17.-17.8 to -20.5	6b	0 to -5
-42.8 to -45.5	2a	-45 to -50	-15.0 to -17.7	7a	5 to 0
-40.0 to -42.7	2b	-40 to -45	-12.3 to -15.0	7b	10 to 5
-37.3 to -40.0	3a	-35 to -40	-9.5 to -12.2	8a	15 to 10
-34.5 to -37.2	3b	-30 to -35	-6.7 to -9.4	8b	20 to 15
-31.7 to -34.4	4a	-25 to -30	-3.9 to -6.6	9a	25 to 20
-28.9 to -31.6	4b	-20 to -25	-1.2 to -3.8	9b	30 to 25
-26.2 to -28.8	5a	-15 to -20	1.6 to -1.1	10a	35 to 30
-23.4 to -26.1	5b	-10 to -15	4.4 to 1.7	10b	40 to 35
-20.6 to -23.3	6a	-5 to -10	4.5 and Above	11	40 and Above

Map: courtesy of the Agricultural Research Service, USDA

175

Glossary

Band pot: A pot commonly used for mail-order roses. The pot is approximately 3 by 5 inches and has bands across the bottom, hence the term *band pot*.

Bare-root rose: A rose that it is sold without soil or packaging around it.

Biodegradable pot: Sometimes also known as a peat pot, it is a pot made from a material designed to break down so you can plant it directly into the soil along with the plant.

Bud and bloom: If a rose has leaves and flowers on it at the time it's being sold, it's called being in "bud and bloom."

Bud eye: Found on the canes and often at the base of a set of leaves, the bud eye is where new stems or canes grow from.

Bud union: The round bulge at the base of the plant above the roots where the canes grow from. This knot is where a bud eye of a particular variety was budded onto a rootstock.

Budded rose: A rose that is budded onto a rootstock. This is opposite of an own-root rose.

Bypass secateurs, clippers, or loppers: The term *bypass* refers to how the cutting blades work. If, when you close the blades, the blades pass by each other to fully close, they are called "bypass." Think of a pair of scissors.

Class of rose: Roses are grouped into classes such as hybrid tea, shrub, floribunda, gallica, and so on. Generally, their ancestry determines their class, but sometimes growth habit is factored in.

Compost: Organic material that has been broken down over time to become almost soillike in consistency. Examples are composted horse manure, mushroom compost, and compost made from kitchen scraps.

Cut-flower roses: Roses that are grown by the florist industry to produce long-stem cut roses for florists.

Deadheading: Removing old flowers to encourage new ones to form. While not necessary to get roses to rebloom, it does cause them to rebloom more quickly.

Dormant: The word *dormant* is used when a rose is not actively growing, as in winter. It is also when a rose for sale is not actively growing. For example, a bare-root rose is dormant.

Dormant pot: Roses sold in biodegradable pots but are not in leaf or flower when you buy them.

Exhibition roses: Roses specifically hybridized to produce blooms to win awards at rose shows. Some do make good garden roses.

Field-grown own-root roses: Roses that are produced by planting own-root cuttings in a field, growing them for one year, and then harvesting them for sale. This method tends to produce larger own-root plants with bigger root systems than those grown solely in pots.

Frost date: The average date on which your first or last frost occurs. The "first average frost date" is at the start of winter, and the "last average frost date" is at the end of winter just before spring.

Garden use: How you can use various roses in your landscape.

Grooming: This is done all season to keep the rose tidy and keep its growth under control. It is a light trimming not nearly as severe as pruning, which is done once a year.

Hybridizing: The act of taking pollen from one rose and putting it on the flower of another rose in an attempt to create a totally new variety.

Knot: The spot above the roots where the canes emerge on an own-root rose. On a budded plant, it is called the bud union.

Large-container roses: Roses sold in 3- to 5-gallon pots in garden centers. They are generally leafed out and in bloom.

Laterals: The flower-bearing side shoots that grow off the main canes of climbing roses and some large shrub roses.

Living soil profile: Soil containing many beneficial microbes that help plants take up nutrients.

Main canes: The long base canes on a climbing rose from which the laterals emerge.

Mulch: Fresh, organic material, like shredded hardwood chips, pine bark, pine needles, and so on, that is used to cover the soil in a garden bed. For roses, hardwood mulch is best.

Mycorrhizal fungi: A specific type of beneficial fungi that help your plants take up nutrients and water from the soil beyond the reach of the actual roots. They are a vital part of a living soil profile.

Own-root rose: A rose that has been propagated by rooting a cutting. Since the root system is the same as the variety above the ground, we say the rose is "on its own roots."

Pillar rose: A climbing rose or large shrub with long canes, with the main canes wrapped around a structure.

Propagation: The act of producing a rose for sale to gardeners. The two common methods are propagating by way of budding (budded roses) or by rooting cuttings (own-root roses).

Pruning: Generally done in late winter to early spring, this is the act of cleaning and cutting back the roses to spur new growth for the upcoming season.

Root ball: The main mass of roots at the base of the plant. It's a combination of the roots and soil that holds together when a plant is taken out of a pot or dug up from the ground.

Root-bound: Any plant that has been in a pot too long and has roots that are tightly wound and knit together.

Rootstock: A variety of rose that is vigorous and is used as a root system for other varieties. A bud eye of a particular variety is budded onto the rootstock.

Rose hips: The bright orange to red berries that show up on most roses in the winter. They contain rose seeds.

Seedlings: The initial small plants that emerge from rose seeds during the hybridizing process.

Spreader/sticker: A product designed to make a liquid spray "stick" to the leaves and better "spread" it on the surface of a plant for longer and better coverage. It's rarely needed for simple garden rose care programs.

Sucker: On a budded rose, it is the cane that can emerge from the rootstock below the bud union. Since it is the rootstock, and not the variety you purchased, it is called a sucker because it "sucks" the nutrients the roots take up before they get to the actual variety you purchased.

Wind rock: When a rose is not firmly anchored in the soil, heavy winds will rock the plant back and forth, tearing the roots and, in some instances, ripping the plant out of the ground.

Resources

Mail-Order Roses: Before You Order

Before you jump into the wonderful world of mail-order roses, here are two websites you should check out. They both provide valuable information before you start visiting nursery websites with all those beautiful photographs.

HELP ME FIND ROSES
www.helpmefind.com/roses

If you are considering buying mail-order roses, this should be your first stop. It is an astonishing website that begins with a database of more than 40,000 roses and 160,000 photographs. From there, you will find ratings by gardeners and—most important for mail-order purposes—a list of rose nurseries that offer the particular rose you are trying to buy. This a great website to browse and learn from. To be impartial, they do not sell ads, but instead rely on memberships and donations.

DAVE'S GARDEN WATCHDOG
http://davesgarden.com/products/gwd

This is an excellent resource for learning about mail-order nurseries. Ratings are provided by nursery customers, and it's a great place to quickly see what others think of a particular nursery.

MAIL-ORDER ROSE NURSERIES AND PRODUCTS

There are a lot of mail-order rose nurseries, and it's impossible to list them all. Following are nurseries I know, have recommended, and have dealt with over the years. They carry a broad range of garden roses. In some instances, not all their roses are garden roses, so do some checking around.

Remember, just because a nursery isn't on the list doesn't mean it isn't good. Ask around on the forums and check out the links I suggested for more information on nurseries you run across.

ANGEL GARDENS
www.angelgardens.com

A Florida-based company that is a good source for own-root garden roses from old to new.

ANTIQUE ROSE EMPORIUM
www.antiqueroseemporium.com

A well-established nursery in Texas that ships nice-sized, 2-gallon own-root roses.

BILTMORE NATURALS
www.biltmorenaturals.com

A result of several years of testing on hundreds of different types of roses, this product line is a probiotic care program for roses. It helps your roses do all the things we talk about in this book to enhance their own inner immune system. I know it works, because I was heavily involved in its development and I've endorsed it!

BURLINGTON ROSE NURSERY
www.burlingtonroses.com

A California-based nursery with a broad selection of garden roses.

CHAMBLEE'S ROSE NURSERY
www.chambleeroses.com

A well-established nursery in Tyler, Texas, that ships high-quality, own-root roses. It's a terrific source for Earth-Kind roses.

COOL ROSES
www.coolroses.com

Based in Florida, this company offers roses on 'Fortuniana' rootstock, which is a rootstock that is sometimes preferred in sandy soils. It is beginning to also offer own-root roses, and its selection of garden roses is steadily increasing.

EDMUNDS' ROSES
www.edmundsroses.com

A Wisconsin-based business that offers a broad range of roses from old to modern, including many garden roses on their own roots and budded.

HEIRLOOM ROSES
www.heirloomroses.com

Based in Oregon, this well-established nursery has been offering garden roses for more than 20 years. It sells own-root roses, and its selection includes many varieties rarely seen in the United States.

NORTHLAND ROSARIUM
www.northlandrosarium.com

Based in Washington, this nursery offers a broad range of garden roses, but its focus is on hardy varieties for colder climates. It primarily sells own-root roses.

ROSES UNLIMITED
www.rosesunlimitedownroot.com

A well-established nursery in South Carolina that has more than 20 years of experience growing and shipping high-quality roses from old to modern, many of them rare. The nursury sells own-root roses.

ROGUE VALLEY ROSES
www.roguevalleyroses.com

This Oregon-based nursery offers a very broad selection of own-root roses from old to modern, rare to not so rare.

WISCONSIN ROSES
www.wiroses.com

If you find yourself wishing to try your hand at exhibiting roses, this nursery is an excellent place to start finding that Queen of Show rose. The roses are grafted onto multiflora and sold as "maiden roses." More information can be found on the website.

Rose Societies

Rose societies are a great place to begin learning more about roses. They have magazines or e-newsletters and generally also websites with good information on roses and rose growing. Many also have local chapters in your area, and these are above all a great source of local knowledge. You can meet and learn from people who garden in your area, and that is invaluable. Start by getting in touch, and joining, the national society and then go join one of the local chapters.

AMERICAN ROSE SOCIETY:
www.ars.org

Founded in 1892, the American Rose Society (ARS) is the oldest single plant horticultural society in America. It has recently revamped its website and magazine (included in the membership), and both are quite good. While ARS used to have a reputation for being an "exhibitors' society," it is striving to fully embrace the broad diversity of rose growing, including organic rose growing and growing roses using many of the methods in this book. Local chapters generally meet once a month, and you should definitely plan to visit one.

ROYAL NATIONAL ROSE SOCIETY
www.rnrs.org

This rose society is the granddaddy of them all. Founded in 1876 and based in England, the RNRS publishes a terrific magazine, and overseas memberships are available. Events are sponsored throughout the United Kingdom during the rose-growing season. The magazine is well worth the membership, even if you can't get across the pond to attend their events.

CANADIAN ROSE SOCIETY
www.canadianrosesociety.org

Canada has a broad range of climates, and growing roses in some of them can be a challenge. The Canadian Rose Society is a great place to learn about growing roses in colder climates but also not-so-cold climates, like that of British Columbia.

HERITAGE ROSES GROUPS
www.theheritagerosesgroup.org

If you are interested in old roses, found roses, or the preservation of unusual roses, this is a great group. It creates an excellent e-newsletter, and in many parts of the country, has very active local chapters. Many of the old roses found growing at old home sites and cemeteries have been preserved and identified through the efforts of this group.

HERITAGE ROSE FOUNDATION
www.heritagerosefoundation.org

This group also works with old roses, and it focuses on identification, genetic research, and the establishment of public gardens of old roses, plus collecting literature, books, and old catalogs of them. The print journal, *Rosa Mundi*, is published three times per year and is simply outstanding.

ROSESHOW.COM
www.roseshow.com

If you are thinking of trying your hand at rose exhibiting, this organization, in addition to the American Rose Society, is a great place to get information on the how, what, where, and why of rose shows.

Useful References

One of the powers of the Internet is that it gives you the ability to connect with people sharing similar interests. From local to worldwide, the reach is vast. And so is the information. While there are many excellent forums out there, here are a few suggestions.

GARDEN WEB ROSES FORUM
http://forums2.gardenweb.com/forums/roses/

This forum is widely visited and a good source if you are seeking rose growers in your area. There are other more specific rose forums for antique roses, propagating, and more. Membership is not required.

LINDA CHALKER-SCOTT, PH.D.
www.theinformedgardener.com

Professor Chalker-Scott is the Extension Horticulturist and Associate Professor at Washington State University, Puyallup Research and Extension Center. She wrote the article "Roses Need Phosphate Fertilizer for Root and Flower Growth" that was referenced on p. 40. Her site is an excellent source of information.

PAUL ZIMMERMAN ROSES FORUM
www.paulzimmermanroses.com/forum/

If the name sounds familiar, that's because this is my own discussion forum. We focus on garden roses and currently have members from more than 20 countries sharing an international wealth of knowledge. On the forum, you can ask questions, post pictures of your garden, get advice from other rose growers around the world, or just share your rose experiences. Membership is not required.

PETER BEALES ROSES FORUM
www.classicroses.co.uk/forum/

This is an excellent discussion forum sponsored by Peter Beales Roses in the United Kingdom. The forum has an international membership, and you will find great advice and information on growing garden roses from old to modern. Membership is not required.

ROSE NURSERY DE BIERKREEK
www.bierkreek.nl/en/home.html

Based in the Netherlands, this EU-certified organic rose nursery is at the cutting edge of organic rose growing. Its website is full of information on growing roses organically, not only for commercial production, but also in your own garden. Versions of the website are available in Dutch, German, Italian, and, luckily for us, English. The nursery doesn't ship roses to the United States, but if you live in Europe, it is an excellent source for top-quality roses of all kinds. It also handle questions on the Paul Zimmerman Roses forum in the "Sustainable" section: http://www.paulzimmermanroses.com/forum/viewforum.php?f=24&sid=cc1d4ab3e807dc3d34b68b537416925d.

Recommended Rose Companies

STAR ROSES AND PLANTS
www.starrosesandplants.com

DAVID AUSTIN ROSES
www.davidaustinroses.com

SPRING MEADOW NURSERY
www.springmeadownursery.com

BAILEY NURSERIES
www.baileynurseries.com

EARTH-KIND
earthkindroses.tamu.edu

KORDES
www.kordesroses.nl

DELBARD ROSES
www.delbard-direct.fr

BILTMORE GARDEN ROSE COLLECTION
www.chambleeroses.com

Photo Credits

© Syl Arena: p. ii; p. 5; p. 150; p. 151 (right); p. 152; p. 153 (except top center); p. 154 (except top left); p. 155 (top left)

© Bailey Nurseries, Inc.: p. 21; 156 (except top left)

© Richard Beals: p. 2

© Biltmore Company: 63 (top)

© Rob Cardillo: p. vi; p. 3; p. 6; pp. 12–13; p. 25; p. 45 (right); pp. 51–53; pp. 55–56; p. 59; p. 96; pp. 104–106; p. 111; p. 113 (bottom); pp. 116–117; p. 120 (bottom); p. 121

© David Austin Roses: p. 96 (top right); p. 68; p. 120 (top); p. 124; p. 125 (top); p. 139 (bottom); p. 140–141; p. 165

© Jon Dodson: p. 8; p. 54; p. 94; p. 98; p. 109; p. 112; p. 131 (bottom left); p. 139 (top)

© Brad Jalbert: p. 66 (right); p. 157 (top and bottom right)

© Kordes Roses/Newflora: p. 163 (bottom right); p. 164

© Meilland International: p. 119; p. 125 (bottom); p. 151 (left); p. 153 (top center); p. 154 (top left)

© Elizabeth Mangino: p. 114

© Clifford Orent: p. 16 (top and center); p. 18; p. 38; p. 61; p. 99; p. 118; p. 138; p. 159; p. 167; p. 168

© Proven Winners: p. 155 (top center and right); p. 156 (top left)

© Rozarium.org: p. 33; p. 57; p. 131 (top right)

Rose Nursery de Bierkreek © Hans van Hage: pp. 46–47; p. 64; pp. 70–71; pp. 72–73; p. 75; p. 76 (bottom) ; p. 77 (top left, top right and bottom); p. 142 (top); p. 144

© Societe nouvelle des Pepinieres & Roseraies Georges Delbard: p. 158

© Star Roses and Plants/Conard Pyle: p. 10; p. 11 (top and bottom); pp. 14–15; p. 16 (bottom); p. 17; p. 20; p. 22; pp. 26–27; p. 58; p. 66 (left and center); p. 85; p. 113 (top); p. 127; p. 128 (top left); p. 131 (bottom right); p. 133; p. 134 (bottom); p. 143; pp. 146–147; p. 151 (top)

© Paul Zimmerman: p. 9 (top left); p. 32; pp. 41–44, p. 45 (left); p. 50; p. 62; p. 63 (bottom); p. 76 (top); p. 77 (center); p. 84; pp. 95; pp. 100–103; p. 110 (top); p. 120 (top); p. 122; p. 128 (top right, bottom left, and bottom right); pp. 129–130; p. 131 (top left); p. 134 (top); pp. 135–136; p. 142 (bottom); p. 145; p. 157 (top center); pp. 160–162; p. 163 (except bottom right)

© Josh Zoodsma: p. 19; p. 24; p. 28; p. 30; p. 35; pp. 36–37;. p. 48; p. 78; pp. 80–81; p. 82; pp. 86–87; pp. 88–89; pp. 90–91; p. 92

Index

If you like this book, you'll love *Fine Gardening*.